I0410953

USDA

United States
Department of
Agriculture

Forest Service

Forest
Products
Laboratory

General
Technical
Report
FPL–GTR–161

# Feasibility of Using Building Deconstruction at Wisconsin's Badger Army Ammunition Plant

## Salvaging Lumber for Reuse in Low-Income Home Construction

Robert H. Falk

# Abstract

The buildings at the Badger Army Ammunition Plant (BAAP) were built in the early years of World War II wholly or partially from wood. The standing timber in these and other military structures is some of the last remaining of our Nation's once vast old-growth forests.

A collaborative effort of government, university, military, and community groups was organized to evaluate the feasibility of using wood-framed building deconstruction at the BAAP to salvage these materials for resale and reuse. Deconstruction is a building dismantlement method based on the separation and recovery of building materials and components for reuse and recycling. Results of this study indicate that the buildings at BAAP contain a wealth of lumber suitable for recovery and reuse. We conclude that nearly 200 wood-framed buildings can be deconstructed immediately and could yield over 4 million board feet of recoverable wood products.

# Acknowledgements

The author acknowledges the contribution of several individuals in helping generate the field data included in this report: Jenna Kunde, WasteCap Wisconsin; Bill Bowman, Austin Habitat for Humanity ReStore; Brad Guy, Hamar Center, Pennsylvania State University; Steve Cramer and Beau Sanders, University of Wisconsin, Madison; Rich Lampo, Steve Cosper, and Tom Napier of the U.S. Army Construction Engineering Research Laboratory.

December 2005

Falk, Robert H. 2005. Feasibility of using building deconstruction at Wisconsin's Badger Army Ammunition Plant: Salvaging lumber for reuse in low-income home construction. Gen. Tech. Rep. FPL-GTR-161. Madison, WI: U.S. Department of Agriculture, Forest Service, Forest Products Laboratory. 35 p.

A limited number of free copies of this publication are available to the public from the Forest Products Laboratory, One Gifford Pinchot Drive, Madison, WI 53726–2398. This publication is also available online at www.fpl.fs.fed.us. Laboratory publications are sent to hundreds of libraries in the United States and elsewhere.

The Forest Products Laboratory is maintained in cooperation with the University of Wisconsin. This article was written and prepared by U.S. Government employees on official time, and it is therefore in the public domain and not subject to copyright.

The use of trade or firm names in this publication is for reader information and does not imply endorsement by the United States Department of Agriculture (USDA) of any product or service.

The USDA prohibits discrimination in all its programs and activities on the basis of race, color, national origin, age, disability, and where applicable, sex, marital status, familial status, parental status, religion, sexual orientation, genetic information, political beliefs, reprisal, or because all or a part of an individual's income is derived from any public assistance program. (Not all prohibited bases apply to all programs.) Persons with disabilities who require alternative means for communication of program information (Braille, large print, audiotape, etc.) should contact USDA's TARGET Center at (202) 720–2600 (voice and TDD). To file a complaint of discrimination, write to USDA, Director, Office of Civil Rights, 1400 Independence Avenue, S.W., Washington, D.C. 20250–9410, or call (800) 795–3272 (voice) or (202) 720–6382 (TDD). USDA is an equal opportunity provider and employer.

# Contents

# Executive Summary

Like many of the U.S. Army's industrial manufacturing and infantry training facilities, the Badger Army Ammunition Plant (BAAP) was built in the early years of World War II. Because metal was in great demand for the war effort, many of the military's buildings were built wholly or partially from wood.

The standing timber in these and other military structures is some of the last remaining of our Nation's once vast old-growth forests. As the results of this report will show, the BAAP is rich in both salvageable and recyclable building materials, especially the structural lumber contained in the many salvageable wood-framed buildings.

This report documents a study to evaluate the feasibility of using wood-framed building deconstruction at the BAAP to salvage these materials for resale and reuse. Deconstruction is a building dismantlement method based on the separation and recovery of building materials and components for reuse and recycling. In contrast to demolition, which focuses on the mechanical reduction of the building for easy transportation and disposal in a landfill, deconstruction allows a greater degree of salvage and reuse of building materials and components. Wood-framed buildings are particularly good candidates for deconstruction because wood members are typically too damaged for reuse after using conventional demolition techniques.

Because of the complexity of the project, a collaborative effort of government, university, military, and community groups was organized. The USDA Forest Products Laboratory (FPL) provided overall management for the project and expertise on the lumber evaluation. United States Army staff at BAAP and the U.S. Army Corps of Engineers, Olin Corporation staff, and Construction Engineering Research Laboratory provided information on the plant infrastructure and expertise on the current disposition and condition of the evaluated buildings. The Civil Engineering Department at the University of Wisconsin–Madison assisted in the actual lumber quantity surveys, and deconstruction experts from the Center for Construction and Environment, University of Florida, and the Austin, Texas, Habitat for Humanity rated candidate buildings for deconstruction feasibility. Finally, WasteCap Wisconsin, Inc., helped find reuse and recycling markets for the materials recoverable at the BAAP.

In this study, a survey of representative building types was made to (1) determine the feasibility of using deconstruction for building removal, (2) quantify the volume of recoverable lumber and timber, and (3) identify markets for the recovered and recyclable materials.

Twenty-eight building types were examined for deconstruction potential. Though these buildings represented only 342 of the 1,444 total buildings at BAAP (24%), they represented about 40% of the total floor area. Further, if actively used buildings and buildings under 1000 ft$^2$ (deemed too small to effectively deconstruct) are not considered, this survey represents over 76% of the total floor area at BAAP.

Results of this study indicate that the buildings at BAAP contain a wealth of lumber suitable for recovery and reuse. We conclude that nearly 200 wood-framed buildings can be deconstructed immediately and could yield over 4 million board feet of recoverable wood products. Assuming future safety evaluation and explosive hazard clearance by the Army, another 700 buildings (50% of total number) have the potential to be removed either wholly or partially using deconstruction. The remaining buildings are either too contaminated with explosive residue for safe removal using deconstruction, are too deteriorated to be salvaged, or are too small or too few in replication to deconstruct cost effectively.

Given the opportunity to develop a non-profit workforce program through Habitat for Humanity and Operation Fresh Start, the buildings were evaluated assuming a high degree of hand deconstruction by unskilled laborers. We assume that the concrete foundations will be removed by others after the deconstruction of the building.

The summary of ratings of the wood-framed buildings that were examined for deconstruction potential is listed below.

| Building number | Building name |
|---|---|
| **Excellent Candidates for Deconstruction** | |
| 1750 | Rest house |
| 3000 | Pulp and cotton warehouses |
| 507 | Warehouse |
| 275 | Warehouse |
| 700 | Compressor house* |
| 1906 | Standard magazines |
| 1932 | Cannon magazines |
| **Moderate Candidates for Deconstruction** | |
| 1885 | Box storehouses |
| 3555 | ACR building |
| 305 | Gun storage and repair |
| 6401 | Bulk storage |
| 6822 | Maintenance shop |
| **Poor Candidates for Deconstruction** | |
| 224 | Ballistic house and range |
| 3022 | Beater house |
| 3036 | Change houses |
| 6586 | Inert storage |
| 6543 | Gatehouse |
| 6864 | Cementing house |

* Presence of lead-based paint on wood members may lower rating to poor.

The buildings most feasible for deconstruction in general are those that have minimal interior partitions and finishes or larger wood members (for example, buildings 3000, 1885, 275, 700). The buildings surveyed can reasonably yield from 40% to 70% wood salvage using deconstruction.

In addition to the salvageable materials, many other recyclables can be recovered. The concrete from the building foundations can be crushed for road-base aggregate, potentially for the reconstruction of Highways 78 and 12. Markets have also been found for the clean scrap wood (broken pieces not suitable for reuse), asphalt roof shingles, and scrap metal. We conclude that over 90% of the building materials can be diverted from the landfill for reuse or recycling from the uncontaminated buildings at BAAP.

From a broader perspective, the immediately available lumber is enough to build nearly 700 new Habitat for Humanity 1,100-ft$^2$ single-family wood-framed homes. Salvage and reuse of the lumber at BAAP will also help conserve our Nation's natural resources and ease harvesting pressure on our existing forest resource. The FPL estimates that reusing the lumber at BAAP will save cutting more than 27,000 trees on 1,000 acres of forestland.

To realize the benefits of deconstruction, time is of the essence. Because the Army is not funded to maintain the buildings at BAAP, many roofs are leaking, and the buildings are deteriorating. This deterioration not only makes deconstruction more costly and less safe, it will rapidly render the wood members useless.

# Feasibility of Using Building Deconstruction at Wisconsin's Badger Army Ammunition Plant

## Salvaging Lumber for Reuse in Low-Income Home Construction

**Robert H. Falk, Research Engineer**
Forest Products Laboratory, Madison, Wisconsin

## Introduction

This report documents a study to evaluate the feasibility of using wood-framed building deconstruction at the Badger Army Ammunition Plant (BAAP) to salvage for resale and reuse building materials, especially the structural lumber contained in the many wood-framed buildings.

Deconstruction is a building dismantlement method based on the separation and recovery of building materials and components for reuse and recycling. In contrast to demolition, which focuses on the mechanical reduction of the building for easy transportation and disposal in a landfill, deconstruction allows a greater degree of salvage and reuse of building materials and components. Wood-framed buildings are particularly good candidates for deconstruction because wood members are typically too damaged for reuse after using conventional demolition techniques.

Using the collective talents of several organizations, a survey of representative building types was made to (1) determine the feasibility of using deconstruction for building removal, (2) quantify the volume of recoverable lumber and timber, (3) identify markets for the recovered and recyclable materials, and (4) identify the effects of chemical contamination on the recovery and reuse of wood materials.

An initial cursory survey of over 100 building types was made to identify buildings with deconstruction potential to be evaluated in a more detailed survey. Twenty-eight building types were carefully examined for quantities of salvageable materials, and deconstruction experts performed a detailed survey and analysis on 10 of these buildings to establish detailed materials take-offs, labor estimates for material removal, and market values of materials.

### Operations and Building Description

The BAAP occupies 7,354 acres in the predominantly rural countryside of Sauk County, Wisconsin, and was constructed in 1942 following the Nation's entry into World War II. The BAAP was an industrial chemical plant that produced a number of chemical-based products for the U.S. Army, including single- and double-base propellant for cannon,

rocket, and small arms ammunition. In the course of producing these products, nitric acid, nitrocellulose, and nitroglycerine were also produced. At full capacity, these products were produced in quantities in the millions of pounds per month. The plant was operated intermittently over a 33-year period, and plant operation was terminated March 1975. At that time, all production facilities and many support functions were placed on standby status, which continued until 1998. The BAAP is currently inactive. In 1998, activities began under the direction of the General Services Administration to excess the property.

Approximately 1,400 buildings are on the property, representing about 100 building types. Seven identical production lines were used at BAAP. As a result, many buildings are of essentially the same design. Most of the buildings are wood-frame on concrete foundations, though concrete, brick, and steel construction are used in some buildings. The buildings on site total over 4 million square feet of floor area. Dimensional (nominal 2-by) lumber was used in constructing many of the buildings, though some use heavy timber construction, concrete, and steel. Although many of the buildings were built as "temporary" structures, they were fully used up to the last production run in 1975. Since then, the installation has been inactive from a production standpoint, and funding for building maintenance stopped in 1999. As a result, many of the buildings are deteriorating, predominately because of leaking roofs.

Each building at BAAP is categorized per Army safety regulations to indicate current explosive hazard. This building classification system is given below:

0    Never contaminated with explosives.
1X    Only routine cleaning after use, substantial explosive residue exists.
3X    Surfaces well cleaned, but less obvious areas may have significant explosive residue. Welding, drilling, sawing, or any type of heat generation not allowed. Can be transferred only to qualified buyers (explosives manufacturers).
5X    No significant amounts of residue remain. No explosive hazard exists. Safe for sale to public.

All production buildings at BAAP are rated 3X. Almost all the buildings use transite (asbestos and Portland cement composite) as a siding material, and many use transite interior wall covering. Many surfaces are painted with lead-based paint. In addition, the interiors contain asbestos cement board and friable asbestos pipe insulation. The buildings are roofed with asphalt shingles, typically a single layer and asbestos free.

## Disposition of Buildings in 2004

Buildings will be turned over to the new landowners ("as-is, where-is") unless there are safety concerns from structural problems or residual explosive contamination, in which case the Army will remove the building. Because of safety concerns, some of the most contaminated buildings (3X) may be burned.

Plexus Scientific Corporation Environmental Services has been retained by the U.S. Army Base Realignment and Closure Office to perform an evaluation of the explosive hazards associated with a group of 17 buildings. These buildings are potentially contaminated with nitrocellulose and nitroglycerin and were selected to reflect different steps in the propellant manufacturing process at BAAP. For information on the proposed burning program, visit the Plexus Scientific Corporation Environmental Services web site (www.plexsci.com/prj/badger/index.shtml).

## A Common Vision

In early 2000, the Sauk County Board of Supervisors acted to establish a locally driven reuse planning process. Efforts to define a future for the BAAP property proved challenging because of the site's unusually rich natural and cultural history, the wide range of potential reuse options, and the complexity of local, state, national, and tribal interests involved. With the assistance of U.S. Congresswoman Tammy Baldwin and funds provided by the U.S. Department of Labor, the Badger Reuse Committee (BRC) was convened. The 21-member BRC included representatives from neighboring communities, local, state, and Federal governments, and the Ho-Chunk Nation. In its mission statement, the BRC charged itself with the task of developing "a common vision for the reuse of the Badger property that can be meaningfully considered and realistically implemented by the appropriate local, state, and federal agencies." Between July 2000 and March 2001, the BRC met 16 times, with additional subcommittee meetings also held in this period.

The *Sauk County Badger Army Ammunition Plant Reuse Plan - Final Report* can be found at their web site (www. co.sauk.wi.us/data/badger/).

The BRC defined nine key values to guide consideration of future uses. A few of the values that are particularly applicable to the building deconstruction process at BAAP include the following:

Value 2. The U.S. Army and/or the Federal government complete the highest quality cleanup of the BAAP's contaminated land, water, building, and infrastructure in a timely manner. Unwanted buildings and infrastructure are removed. Any land transfers do not entail the transfer of unforeseen cleanup responsibilities or liabilities to any party other than the Federal government.

Criterion 2.5: Cleanup activities should provide appropriate educational and research opportunities on the BAAP property.

Criterion 2.6: Salvage operations should preserve materials having historical value and should emphasize recycling of all other materials.

Value 9. Uses and activities at the BAAP property contribute to the area's economic stability and sustainability and have a positive impact on local municipalities.

# Initial Survey of Buildings

To help determine the quantities of lumber and timber materials at BAAP, the Department of Civil Engineering at the University of Wisconsin–Madison surveyed various building types at BAAP. Undergraduate students working on the project completed a cursory survey of over 100 building types and quantified various properties, including the following: number of replicas, dimensional properties, number of floors, production area, type of structural system, and locations of asbestos and painted lumber. Following the cursory survey, a more detailed survey was conducted on 28 building types thought to represent the overall building inventory at BAAP, while holding the most promise for deconstruction (Appendix A). These buildings are listed below:

| Building number | Building name |
| --- | --- |
| 224 | Ballistic house and range |
| 275 | Warehouse |
| 305 | Gun storage and repair |
| 507 | Ingredient warehouse |
| 700 | Compressor house |
| 1600 | Solvent recovery house |
| 1650 | Water dry house |
| 1750 | Rest house |
| 1885 | Box storehouse |
| 1906 | Standard magazine |
| 1932 | Cannon magazine |
| 3000 | Cotton and pulp warehouse |
| 3010 | Cellulose drying house and conveyor (larger) |
| 3019 | Boiling tub house |
| 3022 | Beater house |
| 3024 | Poacher and blender house |
| 3036 | Change house |
| 3044 | Cellulose drying house and conveyor (smaller) |
| 3502 | Ether still house |

| 3516 | Cutting house |
| 3521 | Hydraulic station |
| 3555 | ACR building and duct station |
| 6401 | Bulk storage |
| 6529 | Tractor garage |
| 6543 | Gatehouse |
| 6586 | Inert storage |
| 6822 | Maintenance shop |
| 6864 | Cementing house |

The buildings were chosen using several criteria: (1) they are representative of general building types at BAAP, (2) they are large enough for practical deconstruction, (3) a large number of replicas exist, (4) they have a low contamination rating or have the potential to be decontaminated for deconstruction, and (5) they include larger timbers. Lumber quantities were checked by actual survey and by evaluating blueprints available from Army files.

### Building Survey to Determine Lumber Quantities

We surveyed each building step-by-step, establishing from Army files location, number of replicas, and contamination rating. We looked at the buildings and took notes about the general condition of the foundation, walls, roof, and floors. Special attention was paid to the condition of the siding and roof shingles, as structural damage from wood degradation in wood-framed buildings is typically caused by roof leaks. We also noted the condition and number of windows and doors and whether they were painted. We took digital photos of each building and recorded important details. We noted the presence of exterior porticos, loading and unloading docks, and escape chutes as well as the disposition of the exterior lumber—unpainted, painted, treated, or treated and painted.

We noted the type of construction in the building's interior. In general, most buildings were either light-frame or post-and-beam construction. We counted lumber quantities and sizes and noted the number of rooms and sizes of the rooms as well as the location of asbestos, height of walls, type of flooring, and amount of machinery.

The second phase of the interior survey involved a follow-up calculation of the lumber quantities from the available blueprints. The blueprints were especially helpful for buildings with high ceilings where accurate sizes were difficult to observe or for ceilings and walls that had partitions or plywood coverings.

The individual building information is archived in a Microsoft Access (Microsoft Corporation, Redmond, Washington) database for easy retrieval. This database is available upon request.

### Survey Results

The total number of buildings represented in the survey was 339 (replicas included), which equals about 24% of the total number of buildings and about 37% of the total floor area at BAAP. At first glance, this appears to be a small, and possibly inadequate, picture of the building stock at BAAP. However, many of the buildings are not practical for deconstruction. The actively used buildings at BAAP, including maintenance shops, offices, and fire station, will remain in use for the foreseeable future. Buildings with less than 1,000 ft$^2$ floor area are considered too small for deconstruction because of low salvage value per unit of labor. In addition, some buildings are slated for burning because of their explosive potential. Eliminating these buildings from the count shows that the survey was more representative than it first appears. Eliminating these buildings from the total indicates that the survey represented 36% of the total area of 3X buildings, 76% of the total area of 5X buildings, and 48% of the total building area at BAAP.

Following are some observations from the building surveys:

- The average amount of lumber per building is 42,000 board feet, with a maximum in a single building at 200,000 board feet.

- The exterior transite siding represents the main source of asbestos in the buildings.

- The machinery in the buildings will be an obstacle for deconstruction.

# Deconstruction Feasibility

To determine the feasibility of using deconstruction for building removal at BAAP, two deconstruction experts from the University of Florida and the Austin, Texas, Habitat for Humanity ReStore surveyed a representative sample of building types. They first looked over the principal building types and made a qualitative assessment. They then conducted a quantitative analysis on the more highly rated buildings using detailed materials take-offs, assigned dismantling methods to building assemblies based upon the building type, and estimated salvageable materials. Techniques for building dismantling by assembly ranged from hand deconstruction to mechanized demolition and hybrids of mechanical and hand deconstruction techniques. Only buildings with a 0 or 5X rating were analyzed. Included in this chapter is a description of the methods used for the deconstruction feasibility analysis, the assumptions for the analysis including costs, a description of each building considered in the study along with a proposed method for dismantling, and the detailed deconstruction and salvage cost and quantities estimates for each building.

### Methodology for Study

We created a qualitative survey form for the surveyors to rapidly assess the target buildings and determine those that seemed to justify the additional effort to quantify materials and deconstruction methods. The surveyors visited sites and rated each building on a 1 to 10 scale for deconstruction potential. Several factors were used to scale each building, including the following:

*Site Accessibility* refers to the ability to access the perimeter of the building for people and equipment. High means good access.

*Interior Accessibility* and *Entanglement Factor* refer to the presence or lack of pipes, pads, and miscellaneous elements that make circulation and use of scaffolds problematic. High means good access.

*Safety Factor* refers to the presence or lack of unusual safety concerns such as damaged stairs and holes in the building. High means a dangerous building before work even begins.

*Mobilization Factor* refers to how the building is grouped with others: whether salvage from the building can be moved easily and economically or if the building is one of a type or physically separated from others beyond the reach of a single job site set-up. High means the building will require individual mobilization and cannot be grouped with others.

*Garbage Factor* depends on the amount of miscellaneous debris and garbage in the building. High means garbage in the building would have to removed as part of the preparation.

Buildings that rated a 6 or higher were further analyzed using site measurements and existing construction drawings and deconstruction techniques for which baseline labor and equipment requirements have been established from previous project experience. The material quantification was organized by building assembly. We used a spreadsheet model that translated unit measurements at the building to unit measurements of materials and units of mass and weight for calculating waste disposal. The waste disposal fraction was based on estimates of actual salvage for the building assembly. This fraction can range from 0 (for materials without reuse or recycling potential) to 1 (for individual components that are only salvaged in their entirety, such as a door). The building can be deconstructed using hand labor only; "panelization," where large sections of building are removed intact for disassembly in a staging area; or partial demolition, where portions of the buildings not deemed cost effective for salvage are razed.

The analysis output dollar costs for deconstruction and waste disposal, dollar values of salvage, board feet of estimated lumber salvage, net cost per square feet of building (deconstruction cost minus salvage value), the total mass of the building, the total salvage mass, and the building salvage percentage based on mass. On the basis of net cost, the buildings were then ranked for deconstruction potential in economic terms. Some buildings have larger quantities of salvageable materials but also higher net costs per square feet of building. Many of the buildings studied would appear to be cost-effective for deconstruction based on net cost when compared with demolition.

## Characterization of Buildings

To simplify the analysis and to compare specific buildings with others that were similarly constructed, each building analyzed was assigned a Type number as indicated below.

Type 1 – Building 224 (Fig. 1), one-story with interior walls and concrete walls with concrete slab.

Type 2 – Building 275 (Fig. 2), one-story open warehouse with minimal interior partitions and finishes and raised wood floor.

Type 2 similar – Building 507-4 (Fig. 3), same as Building 275 except rectangular footprint.

Type 2 alternate – Building 6401 (Fig. 4), one-story open warehouse with minimal interior partitions and finishes with concrete slab.

Type 3 – Building 305 (Fig. 5), open warehouse with concrete slab.

Type 4 – Building 700 (Fig. 6), large open warehouse with concrete slab.

Type 5 – Building 1750 (Fig. 7), small one-story rectangular building with interior finish with raised wood floor.

Type 5 alternative – Building 1750-26 (Fig. 8), same as Building 1750 except metal building with concrete slab.

Type 6 – Building 1885-2 (Fig. 9), large open warehouse with minimal to no interiors with concrete slab.

Type 6 similar – Building 3000 (Fig. 10), same as Building 1885.

Type 7 – Building 1906, no berm, small rectangular wood-frame building with concrete slab.

Type 7 alternate – Building 1906 (Fig. 11), bermed, concrete on three sides, wood roof, and concrete slab.

Type 7 similar – Building 1932-32 (Fig. 12), cannon magazine, small rectangular wood-frame building with concrete slab.

Type 8 – Building 3036 (Fig. 13), one-story with interior partitions with concrete slab.

Type 9 – Building 3555 (Fig. 14), large manufacturing building with post-and-beam with concrete slab.

Type 10 – Building 6822 (Fig. 15), one story wood-frame minimal-interior finish with concrete slab.

## Major Assumptions

The analysis performed in this feasibility study is an estimate of potential costs and salvage at BAAP. Because deconstruction is a relatively new building removal method, little data are available for accurate cost predictions. This analysis assumes previous labor and equipment use rates established from pilot deconstruction sites at other Army facilities. To obtain dollar values and make judgments about the dismantling techniques to use, we made the following series of assumptions:

- The cost of disposal is hauling only at $150.00 per haul using 40-yd³ containers. Tipping fee at the landfill is not included as a cost.
- Lumber dollar value is calculated by multiplying linear feet times dimension, or by square foot in the case of sheathing, decking, and flooring.
- Dismantling scenarios are based on an estimated optimal deconstruction process using both hand and mechanical assistance as needed. This includes select demolition on certain parts of a building.
- Recovery for recycling of concrete or asphalt shingles is not included.
- All major processing equipment is removed beforehand and not included in the cost.
- All labor costs and salvage values were estimated based on local Madison and Baraboo, Wisconsin, rates and are used consistently throughout.
- Time is not a constraint.

## Crew Types

As with any construction project, specific tasks may require a crew of laborers with different skills and include the operation and use of heavy equipment. For the purposes of describing techniques that involved more than a set of individual laborers using hand tools, a series of crew types were established. These crew types were then assigned to the appropriate assemblies and techniques. The basic crew types used in this analysis are listed below:

Crew A – Excavator and bobcat (two persons)
Crew B – Skilled laborer(s) (any number of persons)
Crew C – Excavator and two laborers (three persons)
Crew D – Bobcat and one laborer (two persons)
Crew E – Excavator and two laborers (three persons)
Crew F – Excavator and two person-lifts (three persons)
Supervisor [estimated cost: 8% of total labor] (one person)

## Crew Wage and Equipment Costs

Each crew also has a wage rate per hour based on the average of labor wages being paid to each person in the crew. The crew is connected to specific removal techniques and is working simultaneously; therefore the wage per hour is not the addition of each laborer's wage rate but the average of all labor wages paid and the hourly rate paid for the specific piece(s) of heavy equipment used by that crew type. The individual skilled laborer for this project is estimated to cost $18.75 per hour. If a different wage is paid for the actual project, this hourly wage can be changed and reflected in the overall deconstruction analysis. The costs for different crews are listed:

Crew A – $95.63 per hour
Crew B – $18.75 per hour
Crew C – $56.25 per hour
Crew D – $45.00 per hour
Crew E – $52.50 per hour
Crew F – $72.50 per hour
Supervisor – $37.50 per hour

All wages include direct + 25% indirect costs. Figures include equipment rentals pro-rated and are based on weekly rates.

## Crews and Methods

The specific crews and the methods and assemblies that require this crew are listed below.

Crew A – Mechanical demolition of concrete and selective mechanical demolition of walls
Crew B – Hand-deconstruction of any building assembly and process materials
Crew C – Panelize and remove roof sections
Crew D – Separate roof purlins and joists with bobcat
Crew E – Low lift of roof trusses
Crew F – High lift of roof trusses

# Building Descriptions and Recommended Deconstruction Sequence

In our analysis, we compared specific buildings with others that were similarly constructed. The types of buildings that ranked highest for deconstruction feasibility were the following:

1. Type 2 – 275, 6401, similar to 507-4
2. Type 5 – 1750, similar to 1906
3. Type 3 – 305
4. Type 6 – 1885, similar to 3000
5. Type 4 – 700

Following is a description of each type of building and a recommended deconstruction of most buildings.

Figure 1—Type 1–224 ballistic house and range.

Figure 2—Type 2–building 275.

## Building 224 Description

Building 224 (Fig. 1) has large unpainted lumber trusses in the roof with concrete or concrete masonry first-story exterior walls and a large amount of non-salvageable interior finishes.

This building was qualitatively rated 4 for deconstruction potential, and although a low score, it was considered for further analysis for a roof-only deconstruction (Table 1).

## Recommended Deconstruction Sequence for Building 224

- Hand-deconstruct sheathing and shingles
- Hand-demolish ceiling finishes
- Hand-deconstruct trusses
- Salvage storage lockers
- Mechanically demolish exterior walls
- Mechanically demolish slab and foundation(s)

## Building 275 Description

Building 275 (Fig. 2) is a large one-story warehouse with a raised wood floor structure and minimal interior partitions and finishes.

This building was qualitatively rated 8 for deconstruction potential and was considered for further analysis (Table 2).

## Recommended Deconstruction Sequence for Building 275

- Hand-demolish sheathing and shingles
- Hand-deconstruct trusses
- Hand-demolish drywall finishes
- Hand-deconstruct interior wood finishes
- Hand-demolish siding
- Hand-deconstruct exterior studs and sheathing
- Hand-deconstruct wood floor structure

Figure 3—Type 2 similar warehouse 507-4.

Figure 4—Type 2 alternate–6401 bulk storage.

## Building 507-4 Description

Building 507-4 (Fig. 3) was qualitatively rated 8 for deconstruction potential and was considered for further analysis. This building has a raised wood floor structure with minimal interior partitions and finishes.

## Building 6401 Description

Building 6401 (Fig. 4) was qualitatively rated 7 for deconstruction potential and was considered for further analysis (Table 3). This building is identical to 275 warehouse, with the exception that the floor in this building is a raised slab.

### Recommended Deconstruction Sequence for Building 6401

- Hand-demolish roof sheathing and shingles
- Hand-deconstruct trusses
- Hand-deconstruct interior walls
- Hand-demolish siding
- Hand-deconstruct exterior studs and sheathing
- Mechanically demolish floor and foundation(s)

Figure 5—Type 3–305 gun storage and repair.

Figure 6—Type 4–700 compressor house.

## Building 305 Description

Building 305 (Fig. 5) has a light wood-frame exterior, exposed roof structure, 2X sheathing, and minimal interior finishes. The exterior walls have significant numbers of openings and a concrete slab. Building 305 was qualitatively rated 7 for deconstruction potential and was considered for further analysis (Table 4).

## Recommended Deconstruction Sequence for Building 305

- Hand-demolish sheathing and shingles
- Hand-deconstruct trusses
- Hand-deconstruct interior walls
- Hand-demolish siding
- Hand-deconstruct exterior studs and sheathing
- Mechanically demolish floor and foundation(s)

## Building 700 Description

Building 700 (Fig. 6) has an exposed roof structure and walls and large dimensional lumber with minimal interior finish. All wood appears to be covered with lead-based paint. The building has a concrete slab and concrete pits. Building 700 was qualitatively rated 3 for deconstruction potential because of the presence of lead-based paint. Otherwise this building would be highly ranked, and for this reason was considered for further analysis (Table 5).

## Recommended Deconstruction Sequence for Building 700

- Panelize roof for dismantling on the ground
- Lift out trusses and dismantle on the ground
- Gently demolish and pick out timbers and framing lumber
- Mechanically demolish floor and foundation(s)

Figure 7—Type 5–1750 rest house.

Figure 8—Type 5 alternate–1750-26 rest house.

## Building 1750 Description

Building 1750 (Fig. 7) is a small one-story structure with a raised wood floor and interior wood finishes. This building was qualitatively rated 8 for deconstruction potential and was considered for further analysis (Table 6).

## Recommended Deconstruction Sequence for Building 1750

* Hand-demolish sheathing and shingles
* Hand-deconstruct trusses
* Hand-deconstruct interior wood finishes
* Hand-demolish siding
* Hand-deconstruct exterior studs and sheathing
* Hand-deconstruct wood floor structure
* Mechanically demolish foundation(s)

## Building 1750-26 Description

Building 1750-26 (Fig. 8) is a metal frame and cladding on concrete slab. The slab contains mastic that may be an asbestos-containing material. The metal frame and exterior skin are either entirely recyclable or are able to be dismantled and reassembled elsewhere. Building 1750 was qualitatively rated 8 for deconstruction potential but was not considered for further analysis because we lack data on dismantling metal buildings.

Figure 9—Type 6–1885-2 box storehouse.

Figure 10—Type 6 similar–3000 pulp and cotton warehouse.

## Building 1885-2 Description

Building 1885-2 (Fig. 9) has exposed roof and walls and large dimensional lumber columns with minimal interior finishes and concrete slab and stem walls. This building was qualitatively rated 7 for deconstruction potential and was considered for further analysis (Table 7).

## Recommended Deconstruction Sequence for Building 1885-2

- Panelize roofs for building removal
- Mechanically deconstruct and salvage purlins and 2 by 4 sheathing
- Dispose of shingles
- Hand-demolish ceiling finishes
- Lift trusses and hand-deconstruct salvage lumber
- Hand-deconstruct salvage ceiling joists
- Mechanically "soft" demolish and salvage wall studs
- Hand-deconstruct porch
- Mechanically demolish slab and foundation(s)

## Building 3000 Description

Building 3000 (Fig. 10) is on a raised concrete slab and has large dimensional lumber in roof trusses and no interior partitions or debris. This building was qualitatively rated 8 for deconstruction potential and was considered for further analysis.

**Figure 11—Type 7–1906 magazine, standard, berm.**

**Figure 12—Type 7 similar–1932-32 magazine, cannon.**

## Building 1906 Description

Building 1906 (Fig. 11) with a berm has unpainted novelty siding on an interior ceiling, a roof-rafter structure, and wood-framed front wall with a concrete slab. This building was qualitatively rated 9 for deconstruction potential and was considered for further analysis (Table 8).

## Building 1906 with Barricade Description

An alternate type of building 1906 is a small rectangular wood-frame building with concrete slab and no berm (Table 9).

## Recommended Deconstruction Sequence for Building 1906 with 3-sided Berm

- Hand-deconstruct sheathing and shingles
- Hand-deconstruct trusses
- Hand-deconstruct interior wood ceiling finish
- Hand-demolish siding
- Hand-deconstruct exterior studs and sheathing end walls
- Mechanically demolish slab and foundation(s)

## Recommended Deconstruction Sequence for Building 1906 with Barricade

- Hand-deconstruct sheathing and shingles
- Hand-deconstruct trusses
- Hand-deconstruct interior wood wall finish
- Hand-demolish siding
- Hand-deconstruct exterior studs and sheathing
- Mechanically demolish slab and foundation(s)

## Building 1932-32 Description

Building 1932-32 (Fig. 12) interior is entirely unpainted, salvageable lumber with a concrete slab. This would be an excellent building for volunteer or low-skill laborers. This building was qualitatively rated 9 for deconstruction potential and was considered for further analysis.

Figure 13—Type 8–3036 change house.

Figure 14—Type 9–3555 ACR building.

## Building 3036 Description

Building 3036 (Fig. 13) is framed in small dimensional lumber with a drywall ceiling and interior wall and a concrete slab. This building was qualitatively rated 4 for deconstruction potential and was considered for further analysis because of its small scale and potential for un-skilled labor (Table 10).

## Recommended Deconstruction Sequence for Building 3036

• Hand deconstruct sheathing and shingles
• Hand demolish ceiling finishes
• Hand deconstruct trusses
• Salvage storage lockers
• Mechanically demolish exterior walls
• Mechanically demolish slab and foundation(s)

## Building 3555 Description

Building 3555 (Fig. 14) has unpainted large timbers in the roof structure and post-and-beam walls with considerable en-tanglement of various pipes. This building was qualitatively rated 7 for deconstruction potential and was considered for further analysis (Table 11).

## Recommended Deconstruction Sequence for Building 3555

• Panelize roofs and dismantle on the ground
• Lift out trusses and dismantle on the ground
• Hand-deconstruct low roofs and non-truss roof structure
• Demolish walls and pick-out timbers and framing lumber
• Demolish masonry walls and slabs

**Figure 15—Type 10–6822 maintenance shop.**

**Figure 16—3022 beater house.**

## Building 6822 Description

Building 6822 (Fig. 15) has an exposed roof structure with plywood sheathing with a concrete slab. The exterior sheathing is granule asphalt material over suspect friable asbestos fiberboard. This building was qualitatively rated 6 for deconstruction potential and was considered for further analysis.

## Building 3022 Description

Building 3022 (Fig. 16) was qualitatively rated 3 for deconstruction potential and therefore not considered for further analysis. This building has water damage, a high degree of entanglement, and all wood surfaces are painted with what we assume is lead-based paint.

**Figure 17—6586-5 inert storage.**

**Figure 18—6543-5 gatehouse.**

## Building 6586-5 Description

Building 6586-5 (Fig. 17) has three of four exterior walls of poured concrete, the roof structure is salvageable, and sheathing on the one wood-frame wall is asbestos-containing material. Building 6586-5 was qualitatively rated 3 for deconstruction potential and therefore not considered for further analysis.

## Building 6543-5 Description

Building 6543-5 (Fig. 18) is a simple one-story building with a high proportion of interior finishes to salvageable lumber. This could be a good building for volunteer or low-skill laborers. Building 6543-5 was qualitatively rated 4 for deconstruction potential and was not considered for further analysis.

**Figure 19—6864-1 cementing house.**

## Building 6864-1 Description

Building 6864-1 (Fig. 19) has light wood-frame exterior walls and interior walls entirely cast-in-place concrete. It has minimal salvage and was qualitatively rated 2 and therefore not considered for further analysis.

# Markets for Salvaged and Recycled Materials

As an organization with expertise in recycling and materials reuse, WasteCap Wisconsin, Inc., collaborated on this project to help define markets for the materials generated from building removal. WasteCap is a statewide, nonprofit industry-supported 501(c)(3) organization whose primary mission is to provide waste reduction and recycling assistance to businesses. WasteCap assists and encourages companies to effectively drive costs out of their operations through improved solid waste management practices.

In this deconstruction feasibility study, WasteCap's role was to collect information and identify potential reuse or recycling markets for salvaged and waste building materials and develop a listserve to share information, especially among the project team, on the feasibility of using wood-framed building deconstruction for building removal at BAAP.

## Assessments and Presentations

1. March 12, 2003 – WasteCap held a site visit and waste assessment at BAAP with the goal of identifying potential reuse or recycling markets for building materials. Eighteen attendees representing the Wisconsin Department of Natural Resources (DNR), the Construction Material Recycling Association, the USDA Forest Service Forest Products Laboratory (FPL), and potential reuse and recycling markets for building materials from BAAP attended.

2. May 29, 2003 – WasteCap site visit and waste assessment at BAAP and joint presentation with FPL for the Sauk Prairie Conservation Alliance.

3. July 2003 – Site visit and waste assessment at BAAP. We obtained geographic information system data about the site, buildings, and material in the buildings and researched several buildings and materials to determine potential for reuse or recycling.

4. July 29, 2003 – The Badger Study Team met in Madison, Wisconsin, to discuss deconstruction feasibility study project progress.

5. September 16, 2003 – Site visit and waste assessment at BAAP and meeting with several business leaders who can locate businesses able to deconstruct or reuse or recycle materials from BAAP.

## Listserve

The address for the BAAP listserve is badgerdecon@wastecapwi.org. The purpose of this listserve is to send information quickly between the project partners working on the study of the feasibility of deconstruction of BAAP. The listserve may also be used in the future to send information quickly between project partners working on the deconstruction at BAAP. Anyone may send to the

**Figure 20—Possible scenario for contract administration (from Tom Bennwitz, Wisconsin Department of Natural Resources).**

listserve. Names can be added or removed to the BAAP listserve by contacting WasteCap Wisconsin at 414.961.1100 or wastecap@wastecapwi.org.

## Recommendations for Successful Recycling and Reuse

Military bases around the United States have successfully deconstructed buildings for reuse, and many potential models exist for successful reuse of building materials. The following is one model.

1. Determine which buildings to target for deconstruction.

2. Include criteria for deconstruction and materials reuse and recycling in contract documents.

3. Select a coordinator and designate a staff member (typically a general contractor project manager with the cooperation of the site superintendent) to manage the reuse and recycling program.

4. Inventory potential materials for reuse and recycling through photographs, measurements, and tests if needed (for example, send sample of shingles to test for asbestos and send brick samples to potential markets).

5. Identify target materials at the job site that can be recovered from the waste stream.

6. Offer materials to the Badger History Group. Because this property has a strong history, materials should be evaluated for their potential historical significance and reuse by the Badger History Group or other groups that will preserve the historical heritage of the property.

7. Solicit potential end markets for the materials. This can be done using the contacts in this report, advertising materials through photos on web sites, and running ads in the local newspapers and on email lists. Viewings may be held to show potentially interested parties the

materials. On the basis of the Badger Reuse Plan recommendations, we recommend that preference be given to local use of the materials from the site. Generate a list of potentially interested parties and potential end-uses (For example, metal separated for recycling will be handled differently than metal items separated for reuse.). The contractor may want to obtain specific agreements for the reuse or recycling of specific materials (for example, if a company wants to purchase a certain amount of lumber from the site, the lumber can be pre-sold).

8. Write a Deconstruction Waste Management Plan. The contractor will write a plan based on the information gathered during solicitation of potential end markets. The plan will include the following:

   a. Description of building, site, and deconstruction waste management
   b. Description of waste management goals
   c. Meetings to be held with job site crews to discuss waste management
   d. Identification of materials that will be separated for reuse or recycling
   e. Identification of proposed market for each recyclable material (for example, brick separated for reuse as brick instead of being used as clean fill)
   f. Description of materials-handling, separation, and storage requirements for recycling and reuse
   g. Description of waste auditing and documentation procedures

9. Select subcontractors on the basis of the solicitation of end markets. For example, if brick is to be separated for reuse, a subcontractor to handle the brick reuse would be named.

10. Deconstruct, following the deconstruction waste management plan. Recyclables should be taken either to a location onsite for future recycling (shingles and concrete) or to an end market (metals). Reusable items should either be set aside for possible sale (wood, fixtures, signs) or set aside for those organizations that have purchased or to whom the item(s) are being donated.

11. Hold an onsite auction or sell online those items that have been separated for reuse and not yet sold.

12. Document Deconstruction Results. Document cost and savings to the project as a result of deconstruction. Document the project through photographs, interviews, and written materials. Obtain weight, volume, and cost information from hauler(s), general contractor, and subcontractors and track progress. Calculate end-of-project reuse rates, recycling rates, and landfill rates. Calculate the economic effect of the deconstruction with the following data:

   a. The projected cost of disposing all project waste in the landfill
   b. The amount of material landfilled from the project and the total disposal cost by weight and volume
   c. The amount of each material reused and recycled, the cost to reuse and recycle each item by weight and volume, revenue from or cost of recycled or salvaged material
   d. The net total cost or savings of reuse and recycling

13. Celebrate Success. Develop materials related to the project to share this story and its results. Provide information and education through a website and distribute press releases to local and statewide media, trade associations, and other military institutions.

## Material-Specific Recommendations

### Wood

As mentioned earlier, lumber and timber are abundant at BAAP. This material is in several forms and various conditions, which will determine resale markets or recycling options. Both painted and unpainted lumber and timber exist as do preservative-treated members. Smaller wood pieces will be generated in the deconstruction process and can be painted, unpainted, or treated with preservatives. Unpainted lumber and timber can be resold in original form (denailed and end trimmed) and is likely the most marketable of wood materials. Painted wood is more problematic because of the possible presence of lead (see below), though opportunities exist to remill this material, saving the clean wood underneath the paint layer. Preservative-treated wood might be used onsite for a wide range of exterior uses, including curbing, foot-bridges, and decks. Unpainted scrap wood generated in the deconstruction process can be stockpiled and ground for use as mulch. Painted and preservative-treated scrap will have to go to a landfill.

### Regulatory Issues

Wisconsin state law prohibits the sale or transfer of any fixture or other object containing lead-bearing paint that might be placed upon any surface of a dwelling ordinarily accessible to children. Before any painted wood leaves the site, this regulation will need to be considered.

### Processing Options

Preference is given first to reuse, then recycling, then landfilling or burning with energy recovery. If the wood has lead-based paint on it, as the FPL has shown, the wood may be able to be milled for reuse. Any work to remove lead-based paint from wood should be coordinated closely with the Wisconsin DNR and other regulatory agencies, so as not to violate Wisconsin state law pertaining to lead-based paint.

### Marketing Methods for Wood Reuse

1. The building owner can consider offering all materials first to the owners, and then to the Badger History Group

before anything is marketed. (Badger Reuse Plan Value 2, Criterion 2.6. "Salvage operations should preserve materials having historical value and should emphasize recycling of all other materials.")

2. The building owner can consider offering materials next to local businesses and current and former employees of BAAP. (Badger Reuse Plan Value 9. "Uses and activities at the BAAP property contribute to the area's economic stability and have a positive impact on local municipalities.")

3. Any organization that deconstructs the building(s) may be able to use or sell much, if not all, of the wood (see example deconstruction contact below). Note that deconstruction contracts should contain specification language to reuse and recycle targeted materials.

4. The building owner, WasteCap Wisconsin, a broker, contractor, others, or a collaborative effort of several options can market leftover wood for reuse and then recycling. Alternatively, the wood could be auctioned off. WasteCap has experience marketing reusable materials from deconstruction projects.

### Possible Steps

1. Determine location to store usable wood.
2. Ensure that deconstruction results in neat stacks of likesize wood.
3. Inventory available wood for the number of pieces, dimensions of each piece, and condition.
4. Take photos.
5. Market to WasteCap contacts (see Wood Reuse Markets, below), through email, the project web site, newspaper, and radio.
6. Set up (a) time(s) to allow potential buyers to view the wood for sale.
7. Consider public sale onsite.
8. Sell wood via auction, onsite sale, web contact, or phone.

### Recycling

After all available timber is sold (as determined by the owner or seller) and if the timber is untreated and unpainted, with Wisconsin DNR approval it can be ground for use as landscape mulch (see Wood Recycling Markets below).

### Deconstruction Contacts

These companies may be able to deconstruct wood-framed buildings at BAAP:

Kevin Darrah
Darrah/Barns, General Contractor
104 N. Prairie Street
Rockton, IL 61072
Phone: 815.624.4434

Roxanne Seeliger
Deconstruction, Inc.
1010 Walsh Road
Madison, WI 53714
Phone: 608.244.8759

Michael Krause
The Green Institute
2801 21st Avenue South, Suite 110
Minneapolis, MN 55407
Phone: 612.278.7110
Email: michaelk@greeninstitute.org

Bill Bowman
Habitat for Humanity Re-Store
310 Comal, Suite 101
Austin, TX 78702
Office: 512.478.2165 x 201
Mobile: 512.743.5105
Fax: 512.478.9477
Email: billrestore@aol.com

Jen Voichick
Habitat for Humanity Re-Store
208 Cottage Grove Road
Madison, WI 53716
Phone: 608.661.2813
Fax: 608.661.2840
Web site: Habitat for Humanity of Dane County
(www.habitatdane.org)

Bob or Jeff Mast
Marquette County, WI 53926
Phone: 920.394.3072 (Bob)

Liz Covey, Jodi Murphy
Murco Recycling Enterprises
347 N. Kensington
LaGrange Park, IL 60526
Phone: 708.352.4111
Fax: 708.352.4189

Veit & Company, Inc.
14000 Veit Place
Rogers, MN 55374
Phone: 763.428.2242
Fax: 763.428-VEIT (8348)
This company deconstructs buildings for reuse.

Bob Samuaelson
Phone: 312.271.4296
This is a Chicago demolition contractor who deconstructs buildings for reuse.

### Wood Reuse Markets

These companies may be interested in obtaining some of the wood, particularly the timbers, from deconstructed buildings at BAAP for reuse in other buildings. Local companies and individuals typically not considered wood markets may be interested in obtaining some of the wood for reuse. Also, many of the people who worked at BAAP may be interested in obtaining a piece of this historically significant site.

Steve Quick
Barn Again Furniture Company
P.O. Box 320100
Cocoa Beach, FL 32932-0100
Phone: 715.835.5105
Fax: 715.835.0221
This company takes wood from old Wisconsin barns and makes it into furniture.

Lou Host Jablonski
Dell's Architectural Antiques
121 Maple Street
Eau Claire, WI 54703
Phone: 715.834.8872

Design Coalition
2088 Atwood Avenue
Madison, WI 53704
Phone: 608.246.8846
Fax: 608.246.8846
Email: contact@designcoalition.org
This company constructs homes and other buildings with many sustainable materials, including reused wood.

Tom Holmes
Glenville Timberwrights
602 Lake Street
Baraboo, WI 53913
Phone: 608.356.9095 (office)
608.355.9950 (shop)
This local company constructs timber-frame structures with reused wood and is extremely knowledgeable about wood, wood reuse, and markets.

Richard Merlie
Hearthstone Timber Frame dealer
E4827 Horseshoe Road
Spring Green, WI 53588
Phone: 608.588.2851
Fax: 608.588.9181
Email: rlmerlie@execpc.com
Web site: R.L. Merlie Construction Company. 1999. Timber Frame Project (www rlmerlie.com/tfp htm)

Brice Goelke
Interstate Lumber
Neshkoro, WI 54960
Phone: 920.293.4004
This company purchases reclaimed wood and uses it for products, including flooring.

Brett Reichard
Midwest Reclaimed Lumber
1515 Yates Avenue
Beloit, WI 53511
Phone: 608.361.0168

Normerica's Builder–Dealer Program
150 Ram Forest Road
Gormley, Ontario, Canada L0H 1G0
Phone: 1.905.841.3161
Canada and U.S. toll-free phone: 1.800.361.7449
Fax: 905.841.9061
E-mail: info@normerica.com

Emile Smith
Sebastian Specialty Hardwoods
Box 226, Stoney Point Road
Seneca, WI 54654
Phone: 608.734.3157
Email: info@sebwood.com

David Suutala
Phone: 888.492.4652
This timber framer purchases reclaimed wood and uses it to build new buildings.

Swan Timber Frames
4420 Plover Road (Hwy 54)
Wisconsin Rapids, WI 54494
Phone: 715.424.1161
Fax: 715.424.8353
Email: swantmber@tznet.com

Robert Leith
Timber Construction, Inc.
9107 E. Highway 13
South Range, WI 54874
Phone: 715.364.2801
Email: lake-side@centurytel.net
Web site: Timberpeg. 2005 (www.timberpeg.com)

Russ Rastetter
Traditional Woodworks
1679 38th Street
Sommerset, WI 54025
Phone: 800.882.2718
This company purchases reclaimed wood and uses it for products, including flooring.

Trillium Dell Timberworks
1277 Knox Road 1600 North
Knoxville, IL 61448
Phone: 309.221.9380
Fax: 309.289.7921
Email: info@trilliumdell.com
Web site: Trillium Dell Timberworks, 2005
(www.trilliumdell.com/)
This company is a timber framer that uses reclaimed timbers.

Jim Green
Urban Evolutions
Phone: 920.380.4149
Email: info@urbanevolutions.com

### *Wood Recycling Markets*

Wood that is not appropriate to be sold for reuse may be used as landscape mulch. As with wood sold for reuse, wood sold for recycling must be free of lead-based paint and other contaminants. Preservative-treated wood is not recyclable. Most processors can handle some nails. The grinder must ensure that a magnet is used to remove all metal. Wood can be ground and used at BAAP as landscape mulch (likely to be the lowest-cost option) or hauled and marketed off site.

### Grinders

Many companies listed in the local yellow pages offer grinding services. Some are listed below.

Todd Lehman, Vice President Recycling Division
BTL Pallet Corporation
3310 W. Elm Road
Franklin, WI 53132
Phone: 414.761.0220
Cell: 414.801.8446
Fax: 414.761.3566
Email: todd@btlpallet.com
This company grinds and markets scrap wood for landscape mulch.

Kevin Peterson
Construction Debris Management
W11340 740th Avenue
Prescott, WI 54021
Phone: 715.377.6717
Email: kmpeters@pressenter.com
This company grinds scrap wood and other recyclable products (bricks, shingles, etc.).

Ken Patterson or Cynthia Poselenzy
Packer Industries
5800 Riverview Road
Mableton, GA 30126
Phone: 800.818.2899
Email: packerind@aol.com
This company has experience with grinding a variety of construction and demolition products for recycling, including wood as landscape mulch.

Scott Eifler
Resource Recovery Systems, Inc.
1117 Western Drive
Hartford, WI 53027
Phone: 262.673.6801
Toll-free: 800.569.813
Email: scott@rrsinc net
Web site: (www rrsinc net)
This company grinds scrap wood for landscape mulch.

Dave Pellitteri
Pellitteri Waste Systems
7035 Raywood Road
P.O. Box 259426
Madison, WI 53725-9426
Phone: 608.257.4285
Email: davidp@pellitteri.com
Web site: (www.pellitteri.com)
This company can haul scrap wood and have it ground for landscape mulch.

Recycling Markets for Wood
Certified Products
1900 W. Lincoln Avenue
New Berlin, WI 53146
Phone: 262.542.2270

Mark Hanley
Cornerstone of Wisconsin, Inc.
Waukesha, WI 53146
Phone: 262.206.8668

Orlando Olson
Country Recycling
Withee, WI 54498
Phone: 715.229.2342

Robert Walters
Diamond Star
Poynette, WI 53955
Phone: 608.635.4200

Jerry Gruber
Ener-Con
Hartford, WI 53027
Phone: 262.673.8025
This company makes colored mulch.

Tom Helt
Helt Farm
Waunakee, WI 53597
Phone: 608.831.4224 or
608.698.4225

Jeff Mathwig
Pallet One of Wisconsin
310 Portland Road
Waterloo, WI 53594
Phone: 920.478.2082, ext. 23

Timothy Hoeffert
Mobile Reduction Specialists
2707 87th Street
Sturtevant, WI 53177
Phone: 262.886.6777

Norman Arendt
Middleton, WI 53562
Phone: 608.831.5899

Harald Norslien
Norske Woodworks
4738 Hwy 78
Black Earth, WI 53515
Phone: 608.767.3994

Wayne or Pat
Renewed Resources LLC
2780 County Hwy NN
West Bend, WI 53095
Phone: 262.677.3650

Tri-Star Pallet
5023 Farmers Ridge Road
Highland, WI 53543
Phone: 608.929.7777
Email: sales@tristarpallets.com

Anthony Jones
Waste Management, Milwaukee
Franklin, WI 53132
Phone: 414.761.2100

The National Wood Recycling Directory from the American Forest and Paper Association also lists these companies as accepting untreated lumber for recycling.

Johnson Timber Company
9676 N Kruger Road
Hayward, WI 54843
Phone: 715.634.4843

### Additional resources for reuse of wood

Wood Web Lumber Exchange
Web site: Woodweb, Woodworking Industry Information, 2005 (www.woodweb.com)
Business Materials Exchange of Wisconsin
Web site: (www.bmex.org)

### Concrete

Nearly all of the buildings at BAAP have concrete foundations. These foundations, including those where the buildings have been removed by the Army, will be transferred to the new owners. In addition, concrete buildings and other concrete structures and walls are on the property.

### Regulatory Issues

It is unclear whether or not concrete with lead-based paint on it may be recycled or if it must be disposed in a landfill. The owner or general contractors should work with Wisconsin DNR on this issue. The U.S. Army Construction Engineering Research Laboratory (Champaign, Illinois) has worked on this issue (Contact: Steve Cosper).

### Processing and Markets

Concrete is a highly recyclable material and can be ground and reused as aggregate in new concrete, as road sub-base, and back fill. It is most cost-efficient when large volumes are processed at one time. The Highway 12 and 78 road projects adjacent to the site provide a market for most of the concrete at BAAP. Road builders will arrange for the crushing, transportation, and recycling of the concrete. Any concrete not used in the Highway 78 project might be used in other highway projects (Highway 12 or other), for road building (if any) on the BAAP property, for sub-base or fill on site.

### Bricks

Although few buildings (perhaps as few as five—one on each production line) at BAAP are made of brick, brick walls were commonly constructed as fire walls within buildings. In addition, the two power plants (one not in operation) contain large boilers lined in brick.

### Regulatory Issues

Bricks may be reused or recycled under Wisconsin law. However, state law prohibits the sale or transfer of any fixture or other object containing lead-bearing paint that might be placed upon any surface of a dwelling ordinarily accessible to children (Pre-Demolition Environmental Checklist. DNR Publication WA-651-03. Bureau of Waste Management (www.dnr.state.wi.us/org/aw/wm/publications/demolition/predemo.pdf).

### Processing

To assess reuse value, a brick recycler would need a sample of the brick and an estimate of quantity of brick available. Bricks that can be sold for reuse are solid and are a common brick like Chicago Pink or Watertown brick. Brick walls simply need to be knocked down before a brick recycler comes in. Brick recyclers will clean the mortar off of the brick and will stack and transport the bricks for reuse. Bricks will be sold for reuse. Some brick recyclers will pay $40–$60 per 1,000 bricks. Approximately 500 bricks fit on a pallet. Bricks can also be chipped and sold as brick chips for landscape use. Bricks may also be crushed by a concrete recycler as used as aggregate in concrete or sub-base. Some Wisconsin contacts follow:

Antique Brick and Granite Company
Milwaukee, WI 53202
Phone: 414.355.7940
This company can assess the value of bricks, and come in after the brick wall is knocked down to clean the brick and stack, transport, and market it for reuse.

Art Leinweber
The Brickyard, Inc.
3352 S. Clement Avenue
Milwaukee, WI 53207
Phone: 414.481.9600
Fax: 414.481.2770
This company took the bricks from the old Milwaukee County Stadium when it was taken down. They can assess the value of bricks, and come in after the brick wall

is knocked down to clean the brick, stack, transport, and market it for reuse.

Gavin Historical Bricks
2050 Glendale Road
Iowa City, IA 52245
Phone: 319.354.5251
This company is a supplier of authentic antique bricks.

Van Ness Stone
10500 Kinsman Road
Newberry, OH 44065
Phone: 440.338.4444
Web site: (www.vannesstone.com)

### Other markets

The Used Building Material Association has a Brick and Block Exchange where brick can be listed for reuse: (http://build recycle net/a/view/0110 html). Brick yards may be interested in reuse of the brick.

### Asphalt Roofing Shingles

Asphalt shingles are used on all roofs at BAAP except for those in the Ball Powder Production Area. All the buildings in the Ball Powder Production Area (approximately 40 buildings) have concrete asbestos roofs. Historically, all old roofing material was removed when a new roof was installed, so all roofs are single-layer. Additionally, Olin Corporation has maintenance records of when each roof was re-roofed.

### Regulatory Issues

Between 1963 and the mid 1970s, some manufacturers used asbestos in the fiber mat of shingles. In addition, asbestos was commonly used during this time in other asphalt roofing materials (www.shinglerecycling.org).

The disturbance of asbestos is regulated in part by Chapter NR 544, Wisconsin Administrative Code. Prior to beginning a demolition or renovation project, the owner–operator of a structure is required to have the structure inspected for the presence of asbestos. (Pre-Demolition Environmental Checklist. DNR Publication WA-651-03. Bureau of Waste Management (www.dnr.state.wi.us/org/aw/wm/publications/demolition/predemo.pdf). Accessed July 1, 2005).
In Wisconsin, at least one sample from each building must be tested for asbestos before the shingles can be recycled. If the roof has more than one type of shingle, each type of shingle must be tested (personal communication, Tom Stibbe, Wisconsin DNR, Western Central Region).

Three local labs test shingles for asbestos:

John Yakish
Micro Analytical, Inc.
11521 W. North Avenue
Milwaukee, WI 53226
Phone: 414.771.0855
Fax: 414.771.6570

$15 per sample
Provide a container, such as a resealable bag. Results will be sent within five business days.

John Knight
Wisconsin Occupational Health Lab (State Lab)
2601 Agricultural Drive
Madison, WI 53718
Phone: 608.263.6326

EMSL
14375 23rd Avenue North
Plymouth, MN 55447
Phone: 763.449.4922
Fax: 763.449.4924

Fees and turn-around times vary. Fees run between $15 and $50 per sample and turn-around time varies from 24 hours to 10 days. Contact the labs for specific information. Samples should be sent in a resealable container (like a zippable plastic bag).

### Taking Samples

Wisconsin Administrative Code, Chapter NR 477, requires that the structure be inspected for asbestos by an asbestos inspector licensed by the Wisconsin Department of Health and Family Services (DHFS). The DHFS maintains a list of licensed inspectors for the public's review.

### Processing Options

During deconstruction, shingles must be separated from other components such as wood and paper. Waste shingles are typically ground using a horizontal mill, although tub grinders have been used in some applications. The ground shingles are usually screened to achieve a uniform product size (depending on the market), typically 2 in. The ground shingles must be passed under a magnet to remove nails.

### Wisconsin Markets

Several potential markets exist for asphalt shingles. These include hot mix asphalt, cold patch, aggregate road base, and dust control on farmers' properties. At BAAP, shingles could be hauled to an off-site market for processing and marketing. Alternatively, the shingles could be ground to 2 in., nails removed, and the ground shingles stored until they are needed for road building. In particular, up to 50% ground shingle content could be used as a base layer under Highway 78 when it is constructed (personal communication, Tom Bennwitz. Wisconsin Department of Natural Resources, Waste Management Program, South Central Region). The 5% to 10% shingle content can be used in the manufacture of new hot mix asphalt for roads. The companies listed below have experience with shingle recycling. Local asphalt road builders may be able to recycle shingles as well.

Roxanne Seeliger
DeConstruction, Inc.
1010 Walsh Road
Madison, WI 53714
Phone: 608.244.8759
Fax: 608.244.8981
Email: deconstruct@mailbag.com
They deconstruct buildings and recycle a variety of items
and may be able to take shingles for recycling.

Gasser D L Construction
S4383 US Highway 12
Baraboo, WI 53913
Phone: 608.356.3311
They construct roads and have contacted Tom Bennwitz,
Wisconsin Department of Natural Resources, about the
possibility of accepting, processing, and using shingles.

Brian Tippets
La Crosse County Solid Waste Department
6500 State Road 16
La Crosse, WI 54601
Phone: 608.785.9572
Fax: 608.785.6160
Email: btipp@aol.com
La Crosse County Solid Waste Department accepts,
processes, and markets shingles.

Bernie Wenzel
Resource Recovery Team
206 W. Walnut Street
Stratford, WI 54484
Phone: 715.551.4621
Email: berniewenzel@hotmail.com
The Resource Recovery Team accepts, processes, and
markets shingles.

### Other Shingle Recycling Resources

The Minnesota Office of Environmental Assistance web site
contains information about shingle recycling, a tool kit of
resources, fact sheets, research findings, and contacts
(www.moea.state.mn.us/lc/purchasing/shingles.cfm).

The Shingle Recycling web site contains a directory of
markets and other resources and a compilation of test
results for asbestos on shingles that show it to be minimal
(www.shinglerecycling.org).

### Metal

Metal equipment has been used extensively at BAAP. It is
likely that most ferrous metal will be able to be recovered
through any means of building removal—burning, demolition, or deconstruction. We recommend offering materials
first for reuse and then for recycling. Strong local reuse and
recycling markets are available for metal.

### Regulatory Issues

Before removal of metal equipment, potential contamination
will need to be carefully assessed. Additionally, any efforts
to reuse metal coated with lead-based paint should be coordinated with the Wisconsin DHFS and the Wisconsin DNR.

### Processing Options

To reuse the metal, potential end markets for the materials
must be solicited (see Recommendations for Successful Recycling and Reuse, p. 15. Also see Marketing Methods for
Wood Reuse, p. 17). Removal of metal equipment should
be completed as part of an overall building removal contract. Because much of the metal equipment is very large,
it should be removed before deconstruction crews remove
wood, so that the usable wood will not be destroyed in the
process of removing the metal equipment. The contractor
will remove the metal and then it can be offered or sold for
reuse or recycling.

### Markets

There are several local markets for metal, including Del-
aney's Salvage and Dr. Evermore, which are directly across
the street from BAAP. For a list of scrap metal recyclers,
check the local yellow pages or the Wisconsin Recycling
Market Directory at their web site (www.dnr.state.wi.us/org/
aw/wm/Markets/).

### Reusable Items

Unique light fixtures, hand-painted signs, ammunition
boxes, furniture, lockers, and many other relatively small,
reusable, historically significant, and interesting items are
found in the buildings at BAAP. We recommend that these
materials be salvaged for reuse and that they be offered first
to Badger History Group or other organizations that will
preserve their historical heritage.

### Regulatory Issues

No contaminated materials should be sold or given away for
reuse. Regulatory challenges may include codes (electrical
codes, for example), contamination, lead-based paint, and
directives about who is allowed to remove items for reuse.
The Wisconsin DHFS and the Wisconsin DNR can help address the issue of lead-based paint on some reusable items.

## Recommendations for Successful Reuse

Challenges to reuse include labor charges in the removal, the possibility of damaging items in their removal, time availability, and liability concerns. However, many of the strategies below could be successfully used as long as these challenges are addressed.

1. List reusable items on the Business Material Exchange of Wisconsin.

   For materials with potential value, contact the Business Materials Exchange of Wisconsin, a web-based service where companies can list and find materials to give away or acquire.
   Phone: 800.364.3233.
   Web site: (www.bmex.org)

2. Set up a reuse web site.

   WasteCap or others could assist in the creation of a web site and auction. Photos can be placed on a web site created for this project, which depicts the items available for reuse. Individuals or companies can bid for the items and then collect them on designated day(s).

3. Set up a reuse auction.

   WasteCap or others could assist in the creation of an auction for reusable items. An auction could be coordinated whereby time is set aside for people to look at items, bid on items, and remove the items. Liability and other safety issues need to be carefully researched and addressed for both the auction and web site.

4. Use building materials reuse centers and architectural antiques dealers.

   • A list of Wisconsin building materials reuse contacts follows. This list is not inclusive of all places that take materials for reuse in Wisconsin. We recommend calling for prices, hauling arrangements, and any other requirements. Contact local antique dealers and advertise locally first.

   • The Habitat for Humanity ReStore may be able to take and sell many of the materials. Contact Jen Voichick, 608.244.3928, for more information.

   • Individuals from nearby Amish communities may be able to remove items from the building. WasteCap can locate contacts in Wisconsin's Amish community who have experience with reusing materials.

5. Set up site visit(s) with many of the potential reuse or recycling markets.

   WasteCap or others could arrange site visits that would bring together individuals representing reuse and recycling businesses who could bid on the materials from the building.

## Building Materials Reuse Contacts

Pieter Godfrey
1400 E. Park Place
Milwaukee, WI 53211
Mobile: 414.617.8405
Home office: 414.332.8405

Pete Gaitan
Architectural Antiques and Salvage
P.O. Box 926
Grayslake, IL 60030-0926
Phone: 847.343.1044
Fax: 847.223.5775

Habitat for Humanity ReStore
208 Cottage Grove Road
Madison, WI 53716
Phone: 608.661.2813
Fax: 608.661.2840
Web site: (www.habitatdane.org)

HomeSource
3701 W. Lisbon Avenue
Milwaukee, WI 53208
Phone: 414.344.4142

Habitat for Humanity
Sheboygan, WI
Phone: 920.458.3399

The IM Salvage Company
P.O. Box 21621
4025A Loomis Road
Greenfield, WI 53221
Phone: 414.281.8733

Lisbon Storm, Screen and Door, Inc.
5006 W. Lisbon Avenue
Milwaukee, WI 53216
Phone: 414.445.8899

Ralph Middlecamp
St. Vincent de Paul Dig and Save Outlet
1900 S. Park Street
Madison, WI 53713-3230
Phone: 608.250.6370

Tim Hansen
Salvage Heaven
6633 W. National Avenue
West Allis, WI 53214
Phone: 414.329.7170

Jay Weiss
Weiss Brothers Architectural Salvage
113 N. Ingersoll Road
Madison, WI 53703
Phone: 608.256.4988
Email: jweiss@gnic.com

## BAAP Deconstruction Feasibility Collaborators

Bill Bowman
Director of Deconstruction
Austin Habitat for Humanity Re-Store
310 Comal, Suite 101
Austin, TX 78702
Phone: 512.478.2165 ext. 201
Mobile: 512.743.5105
Fax: 512.478.9477
Email: billrestore@ahfh.org

Steve Cosper
U.S. Army Construction Engineering Research Lab
Environmental Process Branch
Champaign, IL 61826
Phone: 217.398.5569
Email: stephen.d.cosper@erdc.usace.army.mil

Steve Cramer, Professor
Department of Civil and Environmental Engineering
University of Wisconsin
Madison, WI 53726
Phone: 608.262.7711
Email: cramer@engr.wisc.edu

Robert H. Falk, Research Engineer
Advanced Housing Research Center
USDA Forest Products Laboratory
One Gifford Pinchot Drive
Madison, WI 53726-2398
Phone: 608.231.9255
Fax: 608.231.9303
Email: rfalk@facstaff.wisc.edu

Brad Guy, Associate Director
Center for Construction and Environment
University of Florida
P.O. Box 115703
Gainesville, FL 32611-5703
Phone: 352.392.7502
Fax: 352.392.9606
Email: guy_brad@yahoo.com

Jenna Kunde, Executive Director
WasteCap Wisconsin, Inc.
2647 N. Stowell Avenue
Milwaukee, WI 53211-4299
Phone: 414.961.1100
Fax: 414.961.1105
Email: jkunde@wastecapwi.org
Web site: (www.wastecapwi.org)

Thomas R. Napier, Research Architect
U.S. Army Corps of Engineers
Engineer Research and Development Center,
Construction Engineering Research Laboratory
P.O. Box 4005
Champaign, IL 61826-9005
Phone: 217.373.3497 or 1-800-USACERL, ext. 3497
Fax: 217.373.7222
Email: thomas.r napier@erdc.usace.army mil

Ken Sandler, Environmental Protection Specialist
U.S. Environmental Protection Agency
(Mail code: 5306w), 1200 Pennsylvania Avenue, NW
Washington, DC 20460
Phone: 703.308.7255
Fax: 703.308.8686
Email: sandler ken@epa.gov

## Other Deconstruction Resources

Pre-Demolition Environmental Checklist. Wisconsin DNR Publication. Bureau of Waste Management. WA-651-03.

Reuse Development Organization web site: (www.redo.org)

Used Building Materials Association web site: (www.ubma. org)

U.S. Environmental Protection Agency – Construction and demolition debris web site including deconstruction information and case studies: (www.epa.gov)

# Conclusions

Many of the buildings at BAAP have materials with strong potential for reuse and recycling: wood, concrete, brick, asphalt roofing shingles, metal, and other reusable items such as signs and fixtures. Strong, economical reuse and recycling markets are available for many of the materials. Although some buildings do not lend themselves to deconstruction because of their small size, contamination, or other factors, at least 200 buildings are immediately suitable as candidates for deconstruction. However, a strong commitment by the new owners, contract language promoting reuse, involvement and buy-in from the local community, diligence in pursuing reuse and recycling markets, and close work with regulatory agencies on regulatory issues surrounding lead-based paint, asbestos, and chemical contamination will be key to ensuring a successful reuse and recycling program at BAAP.

**Table 1—Building 224, 17,136 ft²**

| Building component | Crew | Labor ($) | Disposal | Salvage[a] | BF[b] | Net costs ($) | Cost per ft² ($) | Mass (tons) | Salvage (tons) | Salvage (%) |
|---|---|---|---|---|---|---|---|---|---|---|
| **Full deconstruction method** | | | | | | | | | | |
| Exterior walls | A | 17,793 | 10,174 | 0 | 0 | 27,967 | 1.63 | 678 | 0.00 | 0.00 |
| Interior walls | A | 17,248 | 9,805 | 0 | 0 | 27,053 | 1.58 | 643 | 0.00 | 0.00 |
| Roof 1 | B, D, E | 8,650 | 483 | 2,787 | 16,607 | 6,346 | 0.37 | 39 | 16.18 | 41.47 |
| Gable 1 and 2 | A | 77 | 53 | 0 | 0 | 130 | 0.01 | 2 | 0.00 | 0.00 |
| Ceiling 1 | B | 3,078 | 247 | 780 | 5,957 | 2,545 | 0.15 | 13 | 5.80 | 44.63 |
| Roof 2 | B, D, E | 4,377 | 252 | 2,233 | 9,676 | 2,396 | 0.14 | 21 | 9.42 | 44.88 |
| Ceiling 2 | B | 1,163 | 34 | 440 | 4,724 | 757 | 0.04 | 6 | 4.60 | 76.69 |
| Roof 3 | B, D, E | 7,184 | 416 | 5,162 | 17,466 | 2,438 | 0.14 | 36 | 17.01 | 47.25 |
| Ceiling 3 | B | 3,149 | 211 | 1,527 | 8,600 | 1,833 | 0.11 | 17 | 8.38 | 49.27 |
| Gable 3 | A | 135 | 60 | 0 | 0 | 195 | 0.01 | 4 | 0.00 | 0.00 |
| Gable 3 and 4 | A | 135 | 97 | 0 | 0 | 232 | 0.01 | 4 | 0.00 | 0.00 |
| Roof 4 | B, D, E | 333 | 17 | 127 | 724 | 223 | 0.01 | 1.5 | 0.71 | 47.01 |
| Ceiling 4 | B | 126 | 9 | 60 | 340 | 75 | 0.00 | 0.7 | 0.33 | 47.31 |
| Total | | 63,448 | 21,858 | 13,116 | 64,094 | 72,190 | 4.21 | 1,465 | 62 | 4.26 |
| **Building component method** | | | | | | | | | | |
| Exterior walls | A | 17,793 | 10,174 | 0 | 0 | 27,967 | 1.63 | 678 | 0.00 | 0.00 |
| Interior walls | A | 17,248 | 9,805 | 0 | 0 | 27,053 | 1.58 | 643 | 0.00 | 0.00 |
| Gable ends | A | 347 | 210 | 0 | 0 | 557 | 0.03 | 10 | 0.00 | 0.00 |
| Roofs and ceilings | B, D, E | 28,060 | 1,669 | 13,116 | 64,094 | 16,613 | 0.97 | 134 | 62 | 46.27 |

[a]Does not include contingency, overhead, and profit.
[b]BF, board feet; average wood value $00.20 per board foot.

**Table 2—Building 275, 18,249 ft²**

| Building component | Crew | Labor ($) | Disposal ($) | Salvage ($)[a] | BF[b] | Net costs ($) | Cost per ft² ($) | Mass (tons) | Salvage (tons) | Salvage (%) |
|---|---|---|---|---|---|---|---|---|---|---|
| Full deconstruction method | | | | | | | | | | |
| N wing, N wall | B | 1,337 | 127 | 868 | 5,096 | 596 | 0.03 | 11 | 4.96 | 45.12 |
| N wing, S wall | B | 1,498 | 124 | 736 | 4,740 | 886 | 0.05 | 10 | 4.62 | 46.17 |
| N wing, E wall | B | 197 | 18 | 113 | 672 | 102 | 0.01 | 1.5 | 0.65 | 43.63 |
| E gable | B | 105 | 9 | 64 | 390 | 50 | 0.00 | 0.8 | 0.38 | 47.48 |
| W wall | B | 72 | 2 | 52 | 451 | 22 | 0.00 | 0.5 | 0.44 | 87.85 |
| W gable | B | 105 | 9 | 64 | 390 | 50 | 0.00 | 0.8 | 0.38 | 47.48 |
| S wing, S wall | B | 1,384 | 101 | 862 | 5,067 | 623 | 0.03 | 10.5 | 4.94 | 47.00 |
| S wing, N wall | B | 1,494 | 131 | 739 | 4,398 | 886 | 0.05 | 10 | 4.28 | 42.84 |
| E wall | B | 216 | 23 | 100 | 606 | 139 | 0.01 | 1.6 | 0.59 | 36.89 |
| E gable | B | 105 | 9 | 64 | 390 | 50 | 0.00 | 0.8 | 0.38 | 47.48 |
| S wing, W wall | B | 72 | 2 | 52 | 486 | 22 | 0.00 | 0.6 | 0.47 | 78.89 |
| W gable | B | 105 | 9 | 64 | 390 | 50 | 0.00 | 0.8 | 0.38 | 47.48 |
| Passage, W side | B | 125 | 12 | 72 | 430 | 65 | 0.00 | 0.9 | 0.42 | 46.54 |
| Passage, E side | B | 128 | 13 | 68 | 409 | 73 | 0.00 | 0.95 | 0.40 | 41.93 |
| Bath, E exterior wall | B | 99 | 8 | 44 | 267 | 63 | 0.00 | 0.6 | 0.26 | 43.34 |
| Bath, S exterior wall | B | 155 | 13 | 76 | 457 | 92 | 0.01 | 1 | 0.45 | 44.51 |
| W wall, adjacent office | B | 25 | 1 | 21 | 148 | 5 | 0.00 | 0.2 | 0.14 | 72.08 |
| Office, E exterior wall | B | 51 | 5 | 24 | 147 | 32 | 0.00 | 0.35 | 0.14 | 40.91 |
| Office, W exterior wall | B | 585 | 53 | 232 | 1,413 | 406 | 0.02 | 3.6 | 1.38 | 38.23 |
| Office, S exterior wall | B | 203 | 18 | 85 | 519 | 136 | 0.01 | 1.3 | 0.51 | 38.88 |
| S gable | B | 94 | 7 | 53 | 328 | 48 | 0.00 | 0.65 | 0.32 | 49.15 |
| North exterior wall | B | 203 | 18 | 85 | 519 | 136 | 0.01 | 1.3 | 0.51 | 38.88 |
| North gable | B | 94 | 7 | 53 | 328 | 48 | 0.00 | 0.65 | 0.32 | 49.15 |
| Roof, S wing | B | 13,183 | 303 | 3,936 | 22,832 | 9,550 | 0.52 | 37 | 22.24 | 60.10 |
| Roof, N wing | B | 13,156 | 311 | 4,117 | 24,247 | 9,350 | 0.51 | 39 | 23.62 | 60.55 |
| Roof, office | B | 4,664 | 107 | 1,377 | 7,993 | 3,394 | 0.19 | 13 | 7.79 | 59.89 |
| Roof, passage | B | 357 | 7 | 77 | 425 | 287 | 0.02 | 0.77 | 0.41 | 53.76 |
| Roof, bathroom | B | 426 | 9 | 104 | 616 | 331 | 0.02 | 1 | 0.60 | 60.00 |
| Interior, finished N warehouse | B | 763 | 28 | 1,964 | 4,568 | −1,173 | −0.06 | 5.6 | 4.45 | 79.45 |
| Interior, finished S warehouse | B | 518 | 17 | 1,398 | 2,872 | −863 | −0.05 | 3.5 | 2.80 | 79.92 |
| Interior, finished 3 Office | B | 1,417 | 100 | 2,465 | 2,430 | −948 | −0.05 | 6.9 | 2.37 | 34.30 |
| Interior, finished 4 Office 2 | B | 728 | 51 | 939 | 1,225 | −160 | −0.01 | 3.5 | 1.19 | 34.09 |
| Interior, finished 4a Office 2 | B | 102 | 5 | 52 | 270 | 55 | 0.00 | 0.46 | 0.26 | 57.17 |
| Interior, finished 5 Bath Closet | B | 153 | 25 | 0 | 0 | 178 | 0.01 | 1.13 | 0.00 | 0.00 |
| Wood floors, N wing | B | 5,777 | 265 | 7,590 | 43,885 | −1,548 | −0.08 | 53 | 42.74 | 80.65 |
| Wood floors, S wing | B | 5,777 | 265 | 7,590 | 43,885 | −1,548 | −0.08 | 53 | 42.74 | 80.65 |
| Wood floors, passage | B | 134 | 5 | 292 | 759 | −153 | −0.01 | 0.9 | 0.74 | 82.14 |
| Wood floors, bath | B | 191 | 9 | 652 | 1,539 | −452 | −0.02 | 1.9 | 1.50 | 78.89 |
| Office | B | 1,731 | 63 | 4,377 | 10,507 | −2,583 | −0.14 | 12.8 | 10.23 | 79.95 |
| Total | | 57,529 | 2,289 | 41,521 | 196,094 | 18,297 | 1.00 | 294 | 191 | 65.00 |
| Building component method | | | | | | | | | | |
| Walls and gables | B | 8,452 | 719 | 4,591 | 28,041 | 9,170 | 0.50 | 60.4 | 27.31 | 45.22 |
| Roofs | B | 31,786 | 737 | 9,611 | 56,113 | 22,912 | 1.26 | 91 | 55 | 60.21 |
| Interior finishes | B | 3,681 | 226 | 6,818 | 11,365 | −2,911 | −0.16 | 21 | 11 | 52.49 |
| Floors | B | 13,610 | 607 | 20,501 | 100,575 | −6,284 | −0.34 | 122 | 98 | 80.56 |

[a]Does not include contingency, overhead, and profit.
[b] BF, board feet; Average wood value $00.21 per board foot.

**Table 3—Building 6401, 16,401 ft²**

| Building component | Crew | Labor ($) | Disposal ($) | Salvage ($)a | BFb | Net costs ($) | Cost per ft² ($) | Mass (tons) | Salvage (tons) | Salvage (%) |
|---|---|---|---|---|---|---|---|---|---|---|
| **Full deconstruction method** | | | | | | | | | | |
| E wing, E wall | B | 945 | 89 | 628 | 2,650 | 406 | 0.02 | 7.2 | 2.58 | 35.85 |
| E wing, W wall | B | 963 | 74 | 449 | 2,498 | 588 | 0.04 | 6.1 | 2.43 | 39.89 |
| E wing, N wall | B | 197 | 19 | 105 | 580 | 111 | 0.01 | 1.4 | 0.56 | 40.35 |
| E wing, N gable | B | 101 | 9 | 57 | 318 | 53 | 0.00 | 0.7 | 0.31 | 44.25 |
| E wing, S wall | B | 65 | 2 | 42 | 255 | 25 | 0.00 | 0.4 | 0.25 | 62.09 |
| E wing, S gable | B | 43 | 2 | 31 | 288 | 14 | 0.00 | 0.3 | 0.28 | 93.50 |
| W wing, W wall | B | 945 | 71 | 628 | 3,458 | 388 | 0.02 | 7.2 | 3.37 | 46.78 |
| W wing, E wall | B | 854 | 71 | 456 | 2,278 | 469 | 0.03 | 5.4 | 2.22 | 41.09 |
| W wing, N wall | B | 197 | 19 | 105 | 580 | 111 | 0.01 | 1.4 | 0.56 | 40.35 |
| W wing, N gable | B | 101 | 9 | 57 | 318 | 53 | 0.00 | 0.7 | 0.31 | 44.25 |
| W wing, S wall | B | 65 | 2 | 42 | 363 | 25 | 0.00 | 0.5 | 0.35 | 70.71 |
| W wing, S gable | B | 42 | 2 | 31 | 188 | 13 | 0.00 | 0.3 | 0.18 | 61.04 |
| Passage, S side | B | 121 | 11 | 65 | 361 | 67 | 0.00 | 0.9 | 0.35 | 39.07 |
| Passage, N side | B | 46 | 3 | 27 | 164 | 22 | 0.00 | 0.3 | 0.16 | 53.25 |
| Receiving office, N side | B | 108 | 10 | 60 | 164 | 58 | 0.00 | 0.75 | 0.16 | 21.30 |
| Bath, N exterior wall | B | 96 | 8 | 40 | 225 | 64 | 0.00 | 0.57 | 0.22 | 38.45 |
| Bath E exterior wall | B | 149 | 13 | 68 | 377 | 94 | 0.01 | 0.94 | 0.37 | 39.06 |
| Bath, S wall adjacent office | B | 25 | 1 | 21 | 104 | 5 | 0.00 | 0.13 | 0.10 | 77.92 |
| Office, N exterior wall | B | 55 | 4 | 18 | 104 | 41 | 0.00 | 0.28 | 0.10 | 36.18 |
| Office, S exterior wall | B | 551 | 48 | 199 | 1,115 | 400 | 0.02 | 3 | 1.09 | 36.20 |
| Office, E exterior wall | B | 189 | 17 | 72 | 404 | 134 | 0.01 | 1.1 | 0.39 | 35.77 |
| Office, E gable | B | 89 | 7 | 47 | 265 | 49 | 0.00 | 0.57 | 0.26 | 45.28 |
| Office, W exterior wall | B | 189 | 17 | 72 | 404 | 134 | 0.01 | 1.11 | 0.39 | 35.45 |
| Office, W gable | B | 89 | 7 | 47 | 265 | 49 | 0.00 | 0.57 | 0.26 | 45.28 |
| Roof, E wing | B | 9,801 | 223 | 2,882 | 16,561 | 7,142 | 0.44 | 27 | 16.13 | 59.74 |
| Roof, W wing | B | 9,801 | 223 | 2,882 | 16,561 | 7,142 | 0.44 | 27 | 16.13 | 59.74 |
| Roof, office | B | 3,826 | 88 | 1,182 | 6,840 | 2,732 | 0.17 | 11 | 6.66 | 60.56 |
| Roof, passage/receiving | B | 169 | 39 | 490 | 1,597 | −282 | −0.02 | 2 | 1.56 | 77.77 |
| Roof, bathroom | B | 427 | 9 | 104 | 616 | 332 | 0.02 | 1 | 0.60 | 60.00 |
| Interior, finished W warehouse | B | 69 | 11 | | | 80 | 0.00 | 0.5 | 0.00 | 0.00 |
| Interior, finished, E warehouse | B | 41 | 82 | 0 | 0 | 123 | 0.01 | 0.6 | 0.00 | 0.00 |
| Interior, finished office | B | 523 | 86 | 0 | 0 | 609 | 0.04 | 4 | 0.00 | 0.00 |
| Interior, receiving office | B | 207 | 34 | 0 | 0 | 241 | 0.01 | 1.6 | 0.00 | 0.00 |
| Bath and closet | B | 192 | 26 | 30 | 181 | 188 | 0.01 | 1.4 | 0.18 | 12.59 |
| Total | | 31,281 | 1,336 | 10,937 | 60,082 | 21,680 | 1.32 | 118 | 59 | 49.63 |
| **Building component method** | | | | | | | | | | |
| Foundation/slab | A | 35,695 | 20,357 | 0 | 0 | 56,052 | 3.42 | 1,357 | 0.00 | 0.00 |
| Exterior walls/gables | B | 6,225 | 515 | 3,367 | 17,726 | 3,373 | 0.21 | 42 | 17 | 40.48 |
| Roofs | B | 24,024 | 582 | 7,540 | 42,175 | 17,066 | 1.04 | 68 | 41 | 60.29 |
| Interior finish | B | 1,032 | 239 | 30 | 161 | 1,241 | 0.08 | 8 | 0.16 | 2.00 |

aDoes not include contingency, overhead, and profit.
bBF, board feet; average wood value $00.21 per board foot.

**Table 4—Building 305, 13,592 ft²**

| Building component | Crew | Labor ($) | Disposal ($) | Salvage ($)[a] | BF[b] | Net costs ($) | Cost per ft² ($) | Mass (tons) | Salvage (tons) | Salvage (%) |
|---|---|---|---|---|---|---|---|---|---|---|
| Full deconstruction method | | | | | | | | | | |
| Exterior N1 wall | B | 328 | 29 | 157 | 1,098 | 200 | 0.01 | 2.3 | 1.07 | 46.50 |
| Exterior N1 gable | B | 199 | 18 | 74 | 412 | 143 | 0.01 | 1.2 | 0.40 | 33.44 |
| Exterior W1 wall | B | 667 | 57 | 368 | 2,486 | 356 | 0.03 | 4.9 | 2.42 | 49.42 |
| Exterior N2 wall | B | 162 | 15 | 57 | 314 | 120 | 0.01 | 0.94 | 0.31 | 32.54 |
| Exterior W2 wall | B | 252 | 17 | 232 | 1,484 | 37 | 0.00 | 2.2 | 1.45 | 65.70 |
| Exterior S1 wall | B | 162 | 15 | 57 | 314 | 120 | 0.01 | 0.94 | 0.31 | 32.54 |
| Exterior W3 wall | B | 488 | 44 | 208 | 1,302 | 324 | 0.02 | 3.2 | 1.27 | 39.63 |
| Exterior W3 gable | B | 198 | 18 | 74 | 412 | 142 | 0.01 | 1.2 | 0.40 | 33.44 |
| Exterior S2 wall | B | 1,634 | 147 | 768 | 4,995 | 1,013 | 0.07 | 11.1 | 4.87 | 43.83 |
| Exterior E2 wall | B | 414 | 41 | 126 | 700 | 329 | 0.02 | 2.4 | 0.68 | 28.41 |
| Exterior E2 gable | B | 198 | 18 | 74 | 412 | 142 | 0.01 | 1.2 | 0.40 | 33.44 |
| Exterior N3 wall | B | 1,221 | 106 | 642 | 4,299 | 685 | 0.05 | 8.7 | 4.19 | 48.13 |
| Exterior E1 wall | B | 1,221 | 132 | 492 | 3036 | 861 | 0.06 | 8.5 | 2.96 | 34.79 |
| Roof, NE wing | B | 9,859 | 310 | 5,096 | 30432 | 5,073 | 0.37 | 44.1 | 29.64 | 67.21 |
| Roof, SW wing | B | 12,028 | 385 | 6,412 | 38352 | 6,001 | 0.44 | 55.2 | 37.35 | 67.67 |
| Roof, office 2 and 3 | B | 951 | 20 | 206 | 1,207 | 765 | 0.06 | 2.2 | 1.18 | 53.44 |
| Interior, finished office 1 | B | 195 | 16 | 92 | 611 | 119 | 0.01 | 1.24 | 0.60 | 47.99 |
| Interior finished office 2 | B | 146 | 12 | 50 | 298 | 108 | 0.01 | 0.76 | 0.29 | 38.19 |
| Interior finished office 3 | B | 83 | 6 | 33 | 199 | 56 | 0.00 | 0.43 | 0.19 | 45.08 |
| Interior finished office 4 | B | 268 | 35 | 72 | 440 | 231 | 0.02 | 1.34 | 0.43 | 31.98 |
| Storage room | B | 154 | 5 | 74 | 454 | 85 | 0.01 | 0.64 | 0.44 | 69.09 |
| Small lavatory | B | 102 | 8 | 41 | 250 | 69 | 0.01 | 0.56 | 0.24 | 43.48 |
| Case resizing room | B | 360 | 12 | 137 | 755 | 235 | 0.02 | 1.2 | 0.74 | 61.28 |
| Gun repair room | B | 234 | 9 | 54 | 327 | 189 | 0.01 | 0.7 | 0.32 | 45.50 |
| S gun storage room | B | 374 | 13 | 122 | 677 | 265 | 0.02 | 1.2 | 0.66 | 54.95 |
| Lavatory | B | 42 | 1 | 29 | 176 | 14 | 0.00 | 0.2 | 0.17 | 85.71 |
| Locker room | B | 116 | 3 | 81 | 491 | 38 | 0.00 | 0.6 | 0.48 | 79.71 |
| Loft 1 and 2 | B | 1,257 | 20 | 466 | 3,942 | 811 | 0.06 | 4.65 | 3.84 | 82.57 |
| Total | | 33,313 | 1,512 | 16,294 | 99,875 | 18,531 | 1.36 | 164 | 97 | 59.39 |
| Building component method | | | | | | | | | | |
| Exterior walls | B | 7,144 | 657 | 3,329 | 21,264 | 4,472 | 0.33 | 49 | 21 | 42.86 |
| Roofs | B | 22,838 | 715 | 11,714 | 69,991 | 11,839 | 0.87 | 102 | 68 | 66.67 |
| Interior walls and loft | B | 3,331 | 140 | 1,251 | 8,620 | 2,220 | 0.16 | 14 | 8 | 57.14 |

[a]Does not include contingency, overhead, and profit.
[b]BF, board feet; average wood value $00.16 per board foot.

**Table 5—Building 700, 12,191 ft²**

| Assembly summary and building component | Crew | Labor ($) | Disposal ($) | Salvage ($)[a] | BF[b] | Net costs ($) | Cost per ft² ($) | Mass (tons) | Salvage (tons) | Salvage (%) |
|---|---|---|---|---|---|---|---|---|---|---|
| Full deconstruction method | | | | | | | | | | |
| Exterior wall N | A, B | 1,418 | 738 | 1,135 | 32,808 | 1,021 | 0.08 | 62.8 | 31.95 | 50.88 |
| Exterior wall W | A, B | 598 | 234 | 0 | 2,230 | 832 | 0.07 | 12 | 2.17 | 18.10 |
| Exterior wall W gable | A, B | 68 | 23 | 49 | 277 | 42 | 0.00 | 1.22 | 0.27 | 22.11 |
| Exterior wall S | A, B | 1,366 | 721 | 1,111 | 32,644 | 976 | 0.08 | 62 | 31.80 | 51.28 |
| Exterior wall E | A, B | 607 | 0 | 322 | 2,230 | 285 | 0.02 | 12 | 2.17 | 18.10 |
| Exterior wall E gable | A, B | 68 | 23 | 49 | 277 | 42 | 0.00 | 1.2 | 0.27 | 22.48 |
| Center columns | B | 723 | 5 | 369 | 776 | 359 | 0.03 | 0.94 | 0.76 | 80.41 |
| Roof 1 sheathing | B, D, E | 10,659 | 687 | 2,771 | 15,043 | 8,575 | 0.70 | 47 | 14.65 | 31.17 |
| Roof 1 trusses | B, E | 1,271 | 56 | 3,024 | 9,314 | −1,697 | −0.14 | 11.3 | 9.07 | 80.28 |
| Total | | 16,778 | 2,487 | 8,830 | 95,599 | 10,435 | 0.86 | 210 | 93 | 44.24 |
| Building assembly summary | | | | | | | | | | |
| Exterior walls, columns | A, B | 4,848 | 1,744 | 3,035 | 71,242 | 3,557 | 0.29 | 152 | 69 | 45.39 |
| Roof | B, D, E | 11,930 | 743 | 5,795 | 24,357 | 6,878 | 0.56 | 58 | 24 | 41.38 |

[a]Does not include contingency, overhead, and profit.
[b]Building 700 has lead-based paint on the timbers, so because of potential problems in reusing the wood, no value was assigned to it.

**Table 6—Building 1750, 1,950 ft²**

| Building component | Crew | Labor ($) | Disposal ($) | Salvage ($)[a] | BF[b] | Net costs ($) | Cost per ft² ($) | Mass (tons) | Salvage (tons) | Salvage (%) |
|---|---|---|---|---|---|---|---|---|---|---|
| Full deconstruction method | | | | | | | | | | |
| Floor structure | B | 1,208 | 42 | 1,224 | 8,586 | 26 | 0.01 | 10.1 | 8.36 | 82.80 |
| Exterior wall N | B | 553 | 77 | 123 | 849 | 507 | 0.26 | 4.1 | 0.83 | 20.17 |
| Exterior wall W | B | 137 | 13 | 29 | 204 | 121 | 0.06 | 0.76 | 0.20 | 26.14 |
| W gable | B | 57 | 6 | 22 | 154 | 41 | 0.02 | 0.41 | 0.15 | 36.58 |
| Exterior S wall | B | 432 | 48 | 100 | 692 | 380 | 0.19 | 2.74 | 0.67 | 24.60 |
| Exterior E wall | B | 137 | 13 | 29 | 204 | 121 | 0.06 | 0.76 | 0.20 | 26.14 |
| E gable | B | 57 | 6 | 22 | 154 | 41 | 0.02 | 0.41 | 0.15 | 36.58 |
| Roof | B | 3,510 | 0 | 1,062 | 6,102 | 2,448 | 1.26 | 10 | 5.94 | 59.43 |
| Interior finishes | B | 2,897 | 42 | 3,064 | 4,740 | −125 | −0.06 | 6.3 | 4.62 | 73.28 |
| Total | | 8,988 | 247 | 5,675 | 21,685 | 3,560 | 1.83 | 36 | 21 | 59.36 |
| Building component method | | | | | | | | | | |
| Floor structure | B | 1,208 | 42 | 1,224 | 8,586 | 26 | 0.01 | 10.1 | 8.36 | 82.80 |
| Exterior walls/gables | B | 1,371 | 163 | 325 | 2,257 | 1,211 | 0.62 | 9.18 | 2.20 | 23.97 |
| Roof | B | 3,510 | 0 | 1,062 | 6,102 | 2,448 | 1.26 | 10 | 5.94 | 59.43 |
| Interior finishes | B | 2,897 | 42 | 3,064 | 4,740 | −125 | −0.06 | 6.3 | 4.62 | 73.28 |

[a]Does not include contingency, overhead, and profit.
[b]BF, board feet; average wood value $00.26 per board foot.

**Table 7—Building 1885, 10,400 ft²**

| Building component | Crew | Labor ($) | Disposal ($) | Salvage ($)[a] | BF[b] | Net costs ($) | Cost per ft² ($) | Mass (tons) | Salvage (tons) | Salvage (%) |
|---|---|---|---|---|---|---|---|---|---|---|
| Full deconstruction method | | | | | | | | | | |
|   Exterior E wall | A, B | 951 | 354 | 915 | 3,227 | 390 | 0.04 | 17 | 3.14 | 18.49 |
|   Exterior N wall | A, B | 252 | 95 | 76 | 485 | 271 | 0.03 | 4.5 | 0.47 | 10.50 |
|   N gable | A, B | 104 | 40 | 25 | 163 | 119 | 0.01 | 1.84 | 0.16 | 8.63 |
|   W wall | A, B | 1,041 | 357 | 1,275 | 2,348 | 123 | 0.01 | 17.3 | 2.29 | 13.22 |
|   S wall | A, B | 252 | 95 | 76 | 485 | 271 | 0.03 | 4.5 | 0.47 | 10.50 |
|   S gable | A, B | 104 | 38 | 25 | 163 | 117 | 0.01 | 1.74 | 0.16 | 9.12 |
|   Roof 1 sheathing | B, D, F | 17,647 | 461 | 9,844 | 38,611 | 8,264 | 0.79 | 62.1 | 37.61 | 60.56 |
|   Roof 1 trusses | B, F | 2,337 | 61 | 3,487 | 10,042 | −1,089 | −0.10 | 12.2 | 9.78 | 80.17 |
|   Room 1 interior finished | B | 196 | 6 | 185 | 1,061 | 17 | 0.00 | 1.3 | 1.03 | 79.49 |
|   Room 2 interior finished | B | 1,423 | 116 | 380 | 2,485 | 1,159 | 0.11 | 8.43 | 2.42 | 28.71 |
|   Porch floor | B | 1,357 | 152 | 1,068 | 4,506 | 441 | 0.04 | 10.5 | 4.39 | 41.80 |
|   Stair | B | 25 | 1 | 31 | 133 | −5 | 0.00 | 0.2 | 0.13 | 64.77 |
|   Total | | 22,884 | 1,507 | 17,387 | 63,709 | 7,004 | 0.67 | 142 | 62 | 43.82 |
| Building component method | | | | | | | | | | |
|   Porch | A, B | 1,776 | 377 | 1,099 | 4,639 | 1,054 | 0.10 | 25.7 | 4.52 | 17.59 |
|   Exterior walls | A, B | 2,704 | 979 | 2,392 | 6,871 | 1,291 | 0.12 | 46.88 | 6.69 | 14.27 |
|   Roof | B, D, F | 19,984 | 522 | 13,331 | 48,653 | 7,175 | 0.69 | 74.3 | 47.39 | 63.78 |
|   Interior Finishes | B | 1,619 | 122 | 565 | 3,546 | 1,176 | 0.11 | 10 | 3 | 30.00 |

[a]Does not include contingency, overhead, and profit.
[b]BF, board feet; average wood value $00.28 per board foot.

**Table 8—Building 1906 with 3-sided berm, 1,620 ft²**

| Building component | Crew | Labor ($) | Disposal ($) | Salvage ($)[a] | BF[b] | Net costs ($) | Cost per ft² ($) | Mass (tons) | Salvage (tons) | Salvage (%) |
|---|---|---|---|---|---|---|---|---|---|---|
| Full deconstruction method | | | | | | | | | | |
|   Exterior wall W and gable | B | 213 | 27 | 121 | 736 | 119 | 0.07 | 1.9 | 0.72 | 37.73 |
|   Exterior wall E gable | B | 79 | 7 | 46 | 277 | 40 | 0.02 | 0.6 | 0.27 | 44.97 |
|   Roof | B | 1,960 | 63 | 590 | 4,213 | 1,433 | 0.88 | 7.2 | 4.10 | 56.99 |
|   Interior finished | B | 342 | 12 | 311 | 1,929 | 43 | 0.03 | 2.4 | 1.88 | 78.28 |
|   Total | | 2,594 | 109 | 1,068 | 7,155 | 1,635 | 1.01 | 10 | 6.97 | 68.32 |
| Building assembly summary | | | | | | | | | | |
|   Exterior walls and gables | B | 292 | 34 | 167 | 1,013 | 159 | 0.10 | 3 | 1 | 39.47 |
|   Roof | B | 1,960 | 63 | 590 | 4,213 | 1,433 | 0.88 | 7.2 | 4.10 | 56.99 |
|   Interior finished | B | 342 | 12 | 311 | 1,929 | 43 | 0.03 | 2.4 | 1.88 | 78.28 |

[a]Does not include contingency, overhead, and profit.
[b]BF, board feet; average wood value $00.18 per board foot.

**Table 9—Building 1906 with barricade, 1,972 ft²**

| Building component | Crew | Labor ($) | Disposal ($) | Salvage ($)a | BFb | Net costs ($) | Cost per ft² ($) | Mass (tons) | Salvage (tons) | Salvage (%) |
|---|---|---|---|---|---|---|---|---|---|---|
| Full deconstruction method | | | | | | | | | | |
| Exterior wall N | B | 437 | 45 | 183 | 1,091 | 299 | 0.15 | 3 | 1.06 | 35.42 |
| Exterior wall W | B | 259 | 26 | 109 | 652 | 176 | 0.09 | 1.8 | 0.64 | 35.28 |
| W gable | B | 131 | 13 | 57 | 341 | 87 | 0.04 | 0.9 | 0.33 | 36.90 |
| S wall | B | 437 | 45 | 183 | 1,091 | 299 | 0.15 | 3 | 1.06 | 35.42 |
| E wall | B | 252 | 27 | 104 | 624 | 175 | 0.09 | 1.8 | 0.61 | 33.77 |
| E gable | B | 131 | 13 | 57 | 341 | 87 | 0.04 | 0.9 | 0.33 | 36.90 |
| Roof sheathing | B | 3,079 | 57 | 445 | 1,906 | 2,691 | 1.36 | 4.9 | 1.86 | 37.89 |
| Roof trusses | B | 507 | 33 | 842 | 5,413 | −302 | −0.15 | 6.6 | 5.27 | 79.88 |
| Room interior finished | B | 1,136 | 20 | 564 | 3,098 | 592 | 0.30 | 3.8 | 3.02 | 79.41 |
| Porch exterior walls | B | 11 | 1 | 98 | 181 | −86 | −0.04 | 0.2 | 0.18 | 88.15 |
| Porch roof | B | 85 | 1 | 66 | 194 | 20 | 0.01 | 0.3 | 0.19 | 62.98 |
| Total | | 6,465 | 281 | 2,708 | 14,932 | 4,038 | 2.05 | 27 | 14.54 | 54.47 |
| Building component method | | | | | | | | | | |
| Exterior walls and gables | B | 1,647 | 169 | 693 | 4,140 | 1,123 | 0.57 | 11 | 4 | 36.36 |
| Roof | B | 3,586 | 90 | 1,287 | 7,319 | 2,389 | 1.21 | 12 | 7 | 58.33 |
| Interior finishes | B | 1,136 | 20 | 564 | 3,098 | 592 | 0.30 | 3.8 | 3.02 | 79.41 |
| Porch | B | 96 | 2 | 164 | 375 | −66 | −0.03 | 1 | 0 | 74.00 |

aDoes not include contingency, overhead, and profit.
bBF, board feet; average wood value $00.21 per board foot.

**Table 10—Building 3036, 2,320 ft²**

| Building component | Crew | Labor–equipment ($) | Disposal ($) | Salvage ($)a | BFb | Net costs ($) | Cost per ft² ($) | Mass (tons) | Salvage (tons) | Salvage (%) |
|---|---|---|---|---|---|---|---|---|---|---|
| Full deconstruction method | | | | | | | | | | |
| Interior/Exterior walls | A, B | 657 | 415 | 0 | 0 | 1,072 | 0.46 | 19 | 0.00 | 0.00 |
| Lockers | B | 2,393 | 0 | 3,000 | 6,227 | −607 | −0.26 | 6 | 6.07 | 100.00 |
| Roof | B | 4,200 | 98 | 1,233 | 7,062 | 3,065 | 1.32 | 11.7 | 6.88 | 58.79 |
| Gables | B | 132 | 19 | 82 | 495 | 69 | 0.03 | 1.3 | 0.48 | 37.09 |
| Total | | 7,382 | 532 | 4,315 | 13,784 | 3,599 | 1.55 | 38 | 13 | 35.33 |
| Building component method | | | | | | | | | | |
| Interior/exterior walls | A, B | 657 | 415 | 0 | 0 | 1,072 | 0.46 | 19 | 0.00 | 0.00 |
| Lockers | B | 2,393 | 0 | 3,000 | 6,227 | −607 | −0.26 | 6 | 6.07 | 100.00 |
| Roof/gables | B | 4,332 | 117 | 1,315 | 7,557 | 3,134 | 1.35 | 13 | 7 | 53.85 |

aDoes not include contingency, overhead, and profit.
bBF, board feet; average wood value $00.31 per board foot.

**Table 11—Building 3555, 4,684 ft²**

| Building component | Crew | Labor ($) | Disposal ($) | Salvage ($)[a] | BF[b] | Net costs ($) | Cost per ft² ($) | Mass (tons) | Salvage (tons) | Salvage (%) |
|---|---|---|---|---|---|---|---|---|---|---|
| Full deconstruction method | | | | | | | | | | |
| Exterior wall N 1 | A, B | 420 | 114 | 1,292 | 3,667 | −758 | −0.16 | 9.5 | 3.57 | 37.60 |
| North gable 1 | A, B | 98 | 27 | 169 | 784 | −44 | −0.01 | 1.9 | 0.76 | 40.19 |
| Exterior wall W 1 | A, B | 489 | 155 | 1,627 | 5,821 | −983 | −0.21 | 12.3 | 5.67 | 46.09 |
| Exterior wall W 2 | A, B | 70 | 22 | 122 | 398 | −30 | −0.01 | 1.5 | 0.39 | 25.84 |
| Exterior wall E 3 | A, B | 71 | 22 | 122 | 398 | −29 | −0.01 | 1.5 | 0.39 | 25.84 |
| Exterior wall E 2 | A, B | 489 | 155 | 1,627 | 5,821 | −983 | −0.21 | 12.3 | 5.67 | 46.09 |
| Exterior wall S 3 | A, B | 61 | 16 | 70 | 432 | 7 | 0.00 | 1.1 | 0.42 | 38.25 |
| Exterior wall S 4 | A, B | 61 | 16 | 70 | 432 | 7 | 0.00 | 1.1 | 0.42 | 38.25 |
| Exterior wall S 5 | A, B | 240 | 66 | 637 | 1,736 | −331 | −0.07 | 5.3 | 1.69 | 31.90 |
| S gable 5 | A, B | 36 | 7 | 42 | 275 | 1 | 0.00 | 0.56 | 0.27 | 47.83 |
| Wall 2 N | A, B | 207 | 11 | 471 | 853 | −253 | −0.05 | 2.33 | 0.83 | 35.66 |
| Wall 2 N gable | A, B | 36 | 1 | 42 | 204 | −5 | 0.00 | 0.25 | 0.20 | 79.48 |
| Roof, main sheathing | B, D, F | 7,574 | 190 | 3,672 | 14566 | 4,092 | 0.87 | 23 | 14.19 | 61.68 |
| Roof, main trusses | B, F | 657 | 5 | 278 | 831 | 384 | 0.08 | 1 | 0.81 | 80.94 |
| Roof, S high sheathing | B, D, F | 773 | 20 | 391 | 1571 | 402 | 0.09 | 2.5 | 1.53 | 61.21 |
| Roof, S high structure | B | 88 | 4 | 101 | 621 | −9 | 0.00 | 0.76 | 0.60 | 79.59 |
| Roof, S low W | B | 307 | 4 | 67 | 397 | 244 | 0.05 | 0.54 | 0.39 | 71.61 |
| Roof, S low E | B | 307 | 4 | 67 | 397 | 244 | 0.05 | 0.54 | 0.39 | 71.61 |
| Total | | 11,984 | 839 | 10,867 | 39,204 | 1,956 | 0.42 | 78 | 38.18 | 48.97 |
| Building component method | | | | | | | | | | |
| Slab/masonry | A | 16,324 | 9,315 | 0 | 0 | 25,639 | 5.47 | 621 | 0 | 0.00 |
| Exterior walls | A, B | 2,278 | 612 | 6,291 | 20,821 | −3,401 | −0.73 | 50 | 20 | 40.00 |
| Roofs | B, D, F | 9,706 | 227 | 4,576 | 18,838 | 5,357 | 1.14 | 28 | 18 | 64.29 |

[a]Does not include contingency, overhead, and profit.
[b]BF, board feet; average wood value $00.27 per board foot.

# Appendix A—Example Survey Form

Date:_____11/21/02_____
Surveyor: Brad Guy_____
Building No.: 275_____
Contamination Rating:_____

**Building Dimensions**
Length: See UW Survey form
Width:_____ "_____
Height:_____ "_____
No. of Stories:_____1_____
Roof Slope:_____6/12____

Amount and Location of Asbestos
Suspect:_____na____
Survey: _____na____
Friable: _____na____
Non-friable:_____siding__

Basic Construction
Concrete or Masonry:_____
Wood Frame:_____Yes w/ raised floor_____
Metal Frame:_____

Estimated Materials and Salvage Rate
Roof: 2x10 beams, 2x8 rafter, 2x6 joist @ 24"on half and 2x10 rafter, 2x6 joist on other half
Salvage:_____75_____Recycle:_____
 Lead-Based Paint on Wood:___No____

Floor: 2x6 T&G, 12x12 beams @ 5 bays, 2x12 joist @ 24" 2x6 subfloor
Salvage:_____75_____Recycle:_____
 Lead-Based Paint on Wood:___No____

Interior Finish: 1x6 T&G on perimeter walls
Salvage:_____75_____Recycle:_____
 Lead-Based Paint on Wood:___No____

Exterior Wall:_ 2x4 @ 24", 1x8 @ 45 degree exterior sheathing, horizontal lap siding
Salvage:_____75_____Recycle:_____
 Lead-Based Paint on Wood:___No____

Fixtures: No, some warehouse doors
Salvage:_____N/A____Recycle:_____
 Lead-Based Paint on Wood:___No____

Equipment:_____N/A_____
Salvage:_____Recycle:_____
Lead-Based Paint on Wood:_____

**Overall Salvage Value:** 9/10

Salvage:_____90_____
Recycle:_____5_____
Disposal:_____5_____

**Descriptive Factors**
Building Complexity:              Low
Interior Partitions and Finishes: Low

**Labor**
Volunteer Hand Labor:_____90_____
Professional Hand Labor:___5_____
Mechanical Labor:_____5_____

**Entanglement Factor**
Mechanical:_____0 out of 10_____
Electrical:_____3 out of 10_____
Plumbing:_____0 out of 10_____
Equipment:_____0 out of 10_____
(High # is High Degree of Entanglement)

Site Accessibility:_____High_____
Interior Accessibility:__High_____
Safety Factor:_____Low_____
Mobilization Factor:___High_____
Garbage Factor:_____Medium_____

Notes:_____

**Site Accessibility**: ability to access the perimeter of the building for people and equipment. High means good access.

**Interior Accessibility**: Presence or lack of pipes, pads, miscellaneous elements that make circulation, use of scaffolds, etc. problematic. High means good access.

**Safety Factor**: Presence or lack of unusual safety concerns such as damaged stairs, holes in the building, etc. High means a dangerous building before work even begins.

**Mobilization Factor**: Is the building grouped with others such that there is economy of scale in mobilization or is it one of a type and/or physically separated from others beyond the reach of a single job-site set-up. High means the building will require its own mobilization that cannot be grouped with others.

**Garbage Factor**: How much miscellaneous debris and garbage is in the building that would have to be dealt with as part of the preparation. High means a lot of garbage in the building.

## Current wood retail values

| | | |
|---|---|---|
| 1 by 4 tongue and groove flooring | $1.25 | per square foot |
| 1 by 6 | $0.24 | per square foot |
| 1 by 8 | $0.24 | per square foot |
| 2 by 4 | $0.16 | per linear foot |
| 2 by 6 | $0.20 | per linear foot |
| 2 by 6 tongue and groove decking | $1.25 | per square foot |
| 2 by 8 | $0.27 | per linear foot |
| 2 by 10 | $0.41 | per linear foot |
| 2 by 12 | $0.52 | per linear foot |
| 3 by 6 | $0.66 | per linear foot |
| 3 by 8 | $0.90 | per linear foot |
| 3 by 10 | $1.13 | per linear foot |
| 3 by 12 | $1.35 | per linear foot |
| 4 by 6 | $1.30 | per linear foot |
| 4 by 8 | $1.74 | per linear foot |
| 4 by 10 | $2.16 | per linear foot |
| 4 by 12 | $2.60 | per linear foot |
| 6 by 6 | $1.95 | per linear foot |
| 6 by 8 | $2.60 | per linear foot |
| 6 by 10 | $3.25 | per linear foot |
| 6 by 12 | $3.90 | per linear foot |
| 8 by 8 | $3.47 | per linear foot |
| 8 by 10 | $4.33 | per linear foot |
| 8 by 12 | $5.20 | per linear foot |
| 10 by 12 | $7.50 | per linear foot |
| 12 by 12 | $10.20 | per linear foot |

www.ingramcontent.com/pod-product-compliance
Lightning Source LLC
Chambersburg PA
CBHW080636290526
45790CB00007B/3095